The Musicarta Canon Project
Second Edition

Foreword

Johann Pachelbel's Canon in D major is the ideal place to start learning about chords and how to play a chord sequence. The simple key chords repeat predictably under melodic figures, providing the ideal opportunity for learning about harmony, melody writing and improvisation.

Familiar and delightful, the Canon chord sequence forms the basis of many pieces of popular music, and you will be able to apply the keyboard skills and theory learnt in the Musicarta Canon Project to lots of other chord sequences going forward.

Each module in the Canon Project adds a 'bite-sized' piece to your own unique performance, showing you what to play and how to practice it, with numerous illustrations and full audio and MIDI support.

Studying the Canon also provides a good opportunity to develop your musical ear. Module material coaches your recognition of the Canon chords, and, with practice, you will find yourself being able to tell just by listening what chords are being used in lots of mainstream popular music.

How to use this book

You can use this book simply as a hard-copy work-book, in conjunction with the free-to-air Canon Project material at www.musicarta.com and on Mister Musicarta YouTube.

Alternatively, you can send your proof-of-purchase to webmaster@musicarta.com and claim a free download voucher for the audio and MIDI files which accompany the book.

If you do so, follow the steps in the first section of this book, 'Preparing to Learn', in order to manage your resources efficiently.

About Musicarta

The Canon Project was originally a series of free online piano lessons at www.musicarta.com, a website dedicated to keyboard creativity and popular music keyboard styles. You can find additional interactive Canon Project material on the site via the Canon Project tab on the site navbar, and on the Musicarta YouTube channel.

There are links from Canon Project work-book modules to Musicarta website pages which offer fuller explanations than there is room for in this volume, or to interesting parallel study threads. Musicarta.com hosts lots more chord-based material similar to the Canon Project, which you might like to study in tandem.

Table of contents

THE MUSICARTA CANON PROJECT
PREPARING TO LEARN

Purchase of this Amazon Books version of the Musicarta Canon Project entitles you to a free download of the supporting audio and MIDI files. Redeem your voucher by contacting wemaster@musicarta.com with your purchase transaction details, and use the link to download your supporting files. Then continue working through this Preparing to learn section.

If you are not going to use the supporting digital material, skip forward to the Key of D Major material on page 5 and work from there.

Audio and MIDI support

This module is about organising your resources for efficient learning. A little time spent now will pay off in multiples over your course of study. Tick the checklist boxes as you prepare to start studying the modules.

☐ Make a master Canon Project folder

Nearly every musical example in the Canon Project comes with audio and MIDI support, so you can hear-and-see what to play without having to read music.

Each example has a table below it:

CPA_M1_01	CPM_M1_01

Audio files for musical examples are named in the left hand table cell under the examples. They are always labelled CPA, for Canon Project Audio, then a module number (M1, M2) and a running order number, e.g. CPA_M1_01. Project Supplements have descriptive initials, e.g. VMD for Voice Movement Diagrams – CPA_VMD_01.

MIDI files are numbered the same way but start CPM for Canon Project MIDI.

Your audio and MIDI files are groups in folders by module or supplement in a zipped folder called Canon Project audio + MIDI.

☐ Unzip the Canon Project audio + MIDI file folder.

☐ Put the enclosed Module audio + MIDI folders in your master Canon Project folder.

Your audio files are MP3-encoded. Practically all media players will play them. Leave your audio and MIDI files in the module/supplement folders they came in.

MIDI files are computer-code music files. They can be played in many computer music applications. (Your computer media player will probably be able to play them as base-standard audio files.)

To take full advantage of these MIDI files, Musicarta strongly recommends that you install and learn to use the free MidiPiano 'virtual piano' included in the download.

MidiPiano is simple to use, and shows the music in the MIDI file being performed on a virtual piano keyboard, and scrolling past in a 'piano roll' pane as it plays.

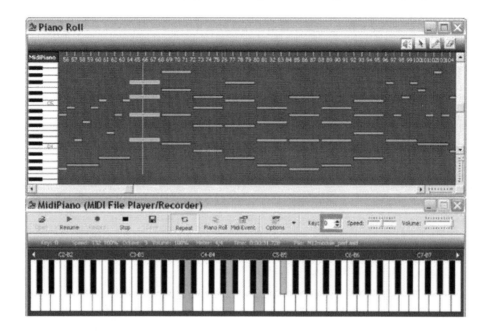

This is a great help in learning and practicing your Canon performances. Musicarta strongly recommends you take the time to install and learn to use MidiPiano. Full instructions and alternative MidiPiano download locations can be found on the Musicarta 'MidiPiano' web page.

MidiPiano is a Windows application only. There are free virtual pianos for all platforms available on the Internet – Synthesia is a good Mac-compatible alternative. If you already have sequencing software like Sonar or Cubase, you can use these to view and listen to MIDI files, but MidiPiano's piano roll display is by far the best option.

☐ Install and learn to operate MidiPiano or Synthesia.

Other audio resources

You will find learning Pachelbel's Canon with Musicarta more rewarding and easier if you have listened to original recordings extensively and have at least one recording to study and play along with. You may already have a recording – check your 'Favourite Classics' CDs.

☐ Recordings sourced and loaded on playback device.

YouTube hosts a useful variety of Canon recordings. Navigate to YouTube and search for Pachelbel's Canon in D. You should listen to them all, more than once and repeatedly, to build up a 'pool' of Canon fragments you're likely to remember.

☐ Canon YouTube performance(s) bookmarked and listened to.

(Musicarta makes no assertions concerning the legality of using the above recordings.)

Keep listening to Canon recordings as you work your way through the course modules. As you go along, the chord sequence and features within the music will become very familiar to you. You will start to realise that you know 'what's going on', and to be able to 'just sit down and play' – but you cannot expect to improvise on a chord sequence you hardly know!

☐ Listen to your Canon recordings regularly and repeatedly.

You can learn a great deal from focussed listening away from the keyboard. Make a playlist of the your commercial Canon recordings and Canon Project backing tracks (see below) on your portable MP3 player so you can study on the move.

☐ Backing track playlist made.

Backing tracks and Audacity

Any commercial recording of the Canon will do as a 'backing track' for you to play along with, but the Musicarta Canon Project also provides a selection of custom-made practice speed backing tracks to support your practice and inspire your improvisations. These are labelled CBT_XX for instrumental backing tracks and CBT_DXX for drum tracks.

Music examples which have a particular recommended backing track have a three-cell table underneath:

| CPA_M1_01 | CPM_M1_01 | CBT_01 |

As well as being a lot of fun, playing along with a recording or backing track is a great stimulus to 'keeping the notes coming'. The Canon is particularly good for this – the piece simply cycles through the same eight chords for its entire duration, so you can join in again easily if you get left behind.

Musicarta highly recommends 'Audacity' (R), a simple, reliable sound editor which can 'loop' (repeat) audio tracks seamlessly. Musicarta backing tracks are edited at a chorus end so that they can repeat properly.

To loop in Audacity, all you have to do is launch the application, 'open' your backing track sound file in the normal way, and press shift+spacebar.

☐ Download and install Audacity and practice 'looping' a backing track.

Windows Media Player will also repeat audio tracks, but not as well. The keyboard shortcut is Control + T; the menu command is in the Play drop-down menu and there is an arrowed circle repeat button on the control bar at the bottom of the player window.

☐ Find the 'repeat' control on your media player.

Windows Media Player's repeat function is fine for repeating an audio performance file over and over until it's 'sunk in' and you can play along.

Most media players can also slow down a performance without changing the pitch. This is a great practice boon – make sure you can manage it.

☐ Learn how to slow down a performance on your media player.

MidiPiano can also slow down MIDI file performances. See above for details.

Practice issues

Musicians are often deterred from practicing by the fact that other members of their household can hear what they are doing. An electronic keyboard with headphones can solve this problem. Moving a real piano out of the family TV lounge is another obvious improvement!

If you have a real piano, you can listen to the Canon backing tracks or recordings on earphones or headphones and still hear yourself play at the same time. If you have an electronic keyboard, you can listen to your backing track on earphones, and put a pair of headphones over the earphones to hear you keyboard, and play along to a backing track in complete privacy.

☐ Earphones and headphones (combination) sourced and tested.

Other Musicarta resources online

Musicarta's 'MisterMusicarta' YouTube channel hosts videos demonstrating Canon Project material. There are also many resources at the main www.musicarta,com site to support your learning and encourage keyboard creativity in all its aspects.

☐ Bookmark www.musicarta,com and the MisterMusicarta video channel.

You do not need to buy any sheet music to follow this course of lessons, but if you are interested, many arrangements of Pachelbel's Canon are freely available on the Internet. (Please note that Musicarta cannot assure the legality of any Internet content.)

☐ Sheet music versions sourced (optional).

The rest of this module explains the key of D major and how to practice the D major scale. If you already know your D major scale/key and have 'prepared to learn' as recommended above, scan the rest of this module quickly and then go straight on to Module One to start building your very own Canon performance.

The key of D major

Pachelbel's Canon is in the key of D major, which uses black keys F sharp and C sharp (the 'key signature').

The music shows the D major key signature. All notes written on the lines or in the spaces shaded in the diagram above (all F's or C's, in fact) are played on black keys F sharp and C sharp, which replace the white-key F's and C's.

This diagram shows one octave of D major scale-tones. It could be anywhere on the keyboard.

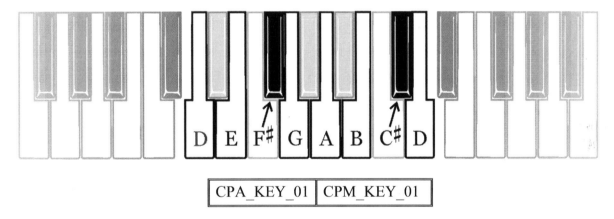

The replaced white keys F and C have been greyed out, along with the black keys you do not use. This is how the well-schooled keyboard player sees the keyboard as soon as he or she sees the two-sharp key signature.

(Note that, if a key signature shows two sharps, they are always F sharp and C sharp. You don't have to count up the lines and spaces to find that out!)

D major scale fingering

It is usual, in keyboard playing, to learn keys by learning the scales. You will learn the Canon much more quickly and enjoy playing more if you do the ground work of learning and playing the D major scale.

Here is our sample octave of D major showing which fingers play which notes. Use keys in the middle of your keyboard to experiment. The left hand will play an octave below the right hand – the next D-to-D set of notes to the left.

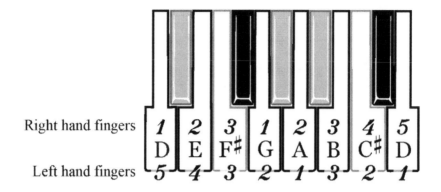

Right hand fingers

Left hand fingers

There are eight notes in the octave but only five fingers on the hand, so we have to play a group of three fingers as well as the handful of five:

Right hand fingers	1	2	3	1	2	3	4	5
	D	E	F♯	G	A	B	C♯	D
Left hand fingers	5	4	3	2	1	3	2	1

This means you have to pass the thumb under or the third finger over to play the full octave.

The right hand – treble clef

Use the 'right hand – treble clef' notes shown on the following keyboard diagram to play the right hand/treble clef scale.

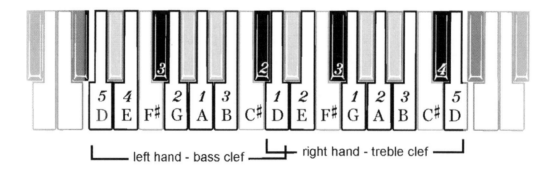

In the music, the black keys are circled to remind you about the key signature, and the thumb-under and third-finger-over places are boxed. (They happen in the same place on the way up and the way down.)

third finger over

thumb under

| CPA_KEY_02 | CPM_M1_02 |

Look at the 'Right hand – going up – thumb under' line in the diagram below to see how it shows the thumb curling under to continue playing the rising scale. See how the curly 'coming down – third finger over' line shows the third finger coming over the thumb to finish playing the descending scale.

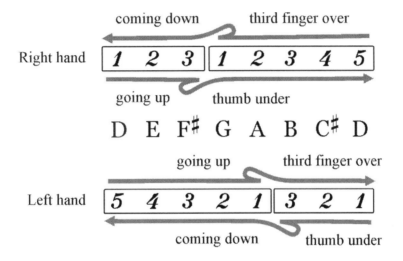

Play an eight-note D major scale with the right hand. Copy the audio and watch MidiPiano play the demonstration file

The left hand – bass clef

The left hand octave starts an octave lower – eight white keys to the left, the next D-to-D group of notes to the left.

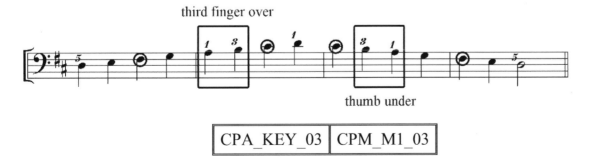

third finger over

thumb under

| CPA_KEY_03 | CPM_M1_03 |

Play a one-octave D major scale with the left hand. Listen to the audio, study the 'going up' and 'coming down' lines in the diagram above and watch MidiPiano play the demonstration file. The important thing is that you start and end on finger five or finger one. (Note that the thumb is 'finger one' in keyboard playing.)

Continue learning the D major scale

It's a good idea to be able to play at least one octave of the D major scale in both hands reliably before starting the actual Canon modules. You should continue practising the D major scale throughout your Canon studies both to reinforce the black-key-for-white-key substitution and increase your finger dexterity. A comprehensive approach to learning scales is presented in the 'Key of D Major' supplement at the end of this e-book.

THIRDS IN THE TREBLE

This is Module One of the Musicarta Canon Project. In this module you will start building your Canon performance by learning the 'thirds in the treble' and playing around with them to produce a performance like this:

> CPA_M1_01

To get the most out of this module, you will need to have installed MidiPiano (or similar) and be able to play your Canon Project MIDI files folder on it. You should have backing track CBT_01 or a classical Canon recording ready and set up to play along with. Start your Canon Project sessions with some D major scale work.

Thirds in the treble

Using just the index fingers (pointing fingers) of both hands, pick out the following string of double notes (thirds) on your keyboard.

| CPA_M1_02 | CPM_M1_02 | CBT_01/any |

The right hand plays the top (higher) note, the left hand plays the bottom (lower) note.

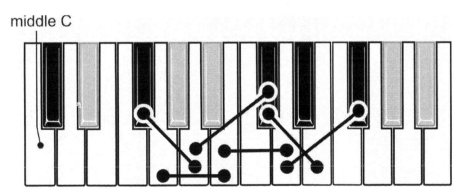

Use the music, the illustration and the audio and the MIDI performance files to help you learn to play the thirds over your backing track. You will sound like this:

| CPA_M1_03 | CPM_M1_03 |

Thirds

These pairs of notes are called thirds because they encompass three note-names – three letters of the musical alphabet.

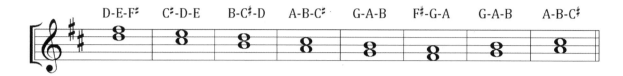

The counting of intervals – pairs of notes – is done by counting the note-names from one note to the other, so you start from one, not zero.

Memorise the string of thirds

Use all the clues you've got to memorise these pairs. One clue is the way the pairs 'slant'. Because the black keys are further away from you, black key/white key pairs slant one way or the other. Here is the music again, with lines above showing the slant of the pair of notes.

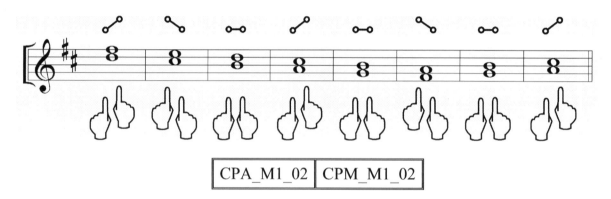

Imagine or draw four dots on your desktop and rehearse the pairs of notes, 'seeing' the black and white keys of the scale of D major as you tap through the string of thirds.

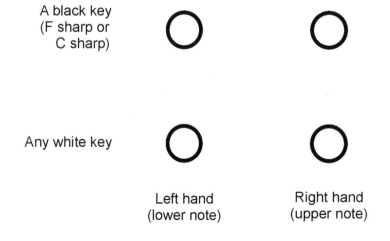

A black key
(F sharp or
C sharp)

Any white key

Left hand
(lower note)

Right hand
(upper note)

Working away from the keyboard like this will help you learn the notes. Then play along with your recording again and watch the slant of the thirds change.

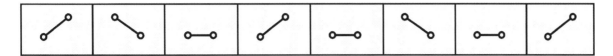

Check your understanding with the audio performance clip again.

| CPA_M1_02 | CPM_M1_02 |

Next, we will explore some simple 'thirds' variations.

Break up the thirds into top and bottom notes

Break up the thirds into top-bottom pairs and play top-bottom-top-bottom in time with the music.

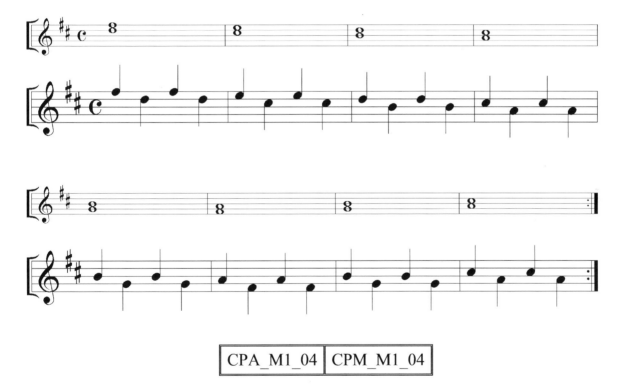

| CPA_M1_04 | CPM_M1_04 |

The original string of thirds is shown reduced just for reference: you only play the larger second and fourth lines.

Play next-door scale tones in the right hand

We can easily embellish our thirds using next-door scale tones in the right hand. The right hand uses the D major scale tone immediately above its 'third' tone, like this:

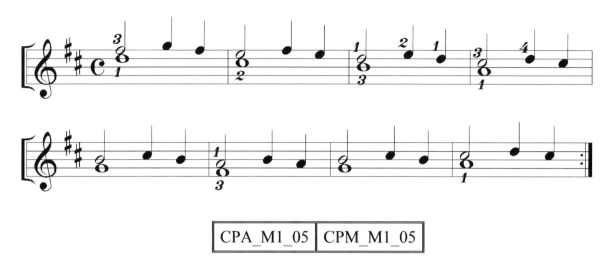

| CPA_M1_05 | CPM_M1_05 |

Once you start playing like this, you can't keep using just one finger in the right hand. The music gives a suggested fingering. You don't have to follow it exactly, but you should avoid running out of fingers or using your thumb on a black key.

The audio and MIDI performance files from here on are slowed down to practice tempo to help you learn the pattern. Remember, you can slow down the performance still more in MidiPiano while you're learning.

Give the pattern a different rhythm

We can make this pattern more interesting by making our next-door scale tone shorter.

| CPA_M1_06 | CPM_M1_06 |

Note the right hand 'tweak' in the last bar before the chords start repeating. 'Formula' patterns often sound better if you change a note or two here or there (the 'tweak').

Double the number of left hand notes

We can continue to develop the pattern by doubling up the left hand notes.

| CPA_M1_07 | CPM_M1_07 |

Look out for more tweaks in bar 7 (right hand) and bar 8 (left hand).

Audio challenge: Further Variations

Listen to these two audio clips and try to play the music you hear.

| CPA_M1_08 | CPM_M1_08 |

| CPA_M1_09 | CPM_M1_09 |

The first variation has fewer notes in the right hand, the second one has more, but always the same next-door-above scale tones. See if you can play the variations from just the audio clips, or use MidiPiano to watch what happens, and copy.

To check your work, or just to see the written-out music, go to the Module One 'Answers' section.

Playing by ear – just 'have a go'!

Playing by ear is a skill you build – and everybody has to start somewhere! The audio challenges in the Canon Project offer a great chance to work on your playing-by-ear, because the music for you to try copying is always similar to the music you have just played or heard. Don't be discouraged if you don't 'get it right' first time! Every time you make a mistake and try again, you are laying the foundations of your own long-term accomplishment.

You cannot be creative and at the same time insist on knowing in advance that the next thing you play will be 'right'. Creativity is inseparable from the likelihood of making mistakes. And it's an open secret that lots of attractive music springs from 'happy accidents' stumbled upon just trying things out at the keyboard.

Here are two more patterns separated out from the module performance:

CPA_M1_10	CPA_M1_10

CPA_M1_11	CPA_M1_11

Try playing them by ear, or watch the MIDI files in MidiPiano for the actual notes.

You can use any of the instrumental backing tracks to practice these thirds patterns over. Play the backing track in Windows Media Player with 'repeat' switched on, or load it into Audacity and press shift+spacebar to get the 'loop' (repeat) going.

Here is the module performance again, with the MIDI file reference number.

CPA_M1_01	CPM_M1_01

Practice the patterns until you can play along with the performance files and your backing track, then try playing the patterns up to speed with your classical recording in the background.

With practice, you will be able to play all these thirds-based treble variations. Get creative and put together your own performance by combining the elements in a different order, along with any other variations you might have discovered.

When you're ready, go on to Module Two, where you learn the bass line – the roots of the Canon chords. You don't have to complete every single task to move forward!

Keep practising your scales!

All music is in a certain key. At the piano, this means using some of the black keys instead of some of the white keys. These black keys are indicated in the key signature at the start of a line of keyboard music.

To be the musician you want to be, you will need to be able to play in several keys, and playing scales is a tried and tested way of learning the right piano keys to use. Learning scales is not just another hoop to jump through – it's about becoming a better, freer musician.

The Canon is in D major, which is an easy scale to learn and a model for all the 'sharp key' scales (G, D, A, and E majors). Ideally, you would start all your Canon Project study sessions with some D major scale practice. The Key of D Major supplement at the back of the book contains a wealth of scale practice patterns to keep your practice interesting and progressively build your ability.

THE BASS LINE

If you listen to any classical recording of the Pachelbel Canon, one of the first things you notice is the string of eight low notes – the 'bass line'. In this module, you will learn to play the bass line with your left hand and the thirds from Module One with your right hand, combining them in a performance like this:

CPA_M2_01

To get the most out of this module, you will need to locate your Canon Project MIDI file folder and play the numbered MIDI files on MidiPiano. You should also have a Musicarta backing track and/or a classical Canon recording to play along with. You should also be able to play a one-octave D major scale, hands together,

The bass line

One of the first things you hear in most recordings of the Pachelbel Canon is this line of eight bass notes:

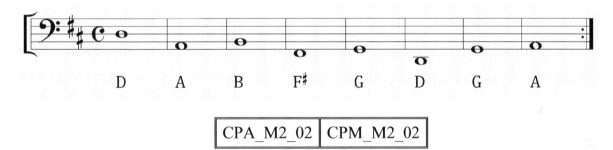

D A B F♯ G D G A

CPA_M2_02 | CPM_M2_02

This is the 'bass line'. It uses these six D major scale tones:

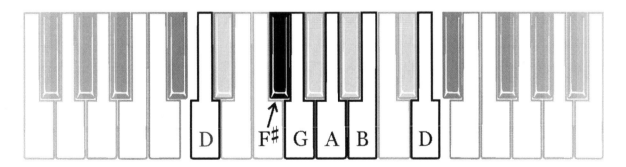

Listen to your recording to hear the bass line, then pick out the notes from the music and the keyboard illustration. Play along with your selected recording.

Further on in this module, you are going to play the bass line in the left hand and the thirds from Module One in the right hand. To do this, it is essential that you know the bass line by heart, even if you still use written music as a reminder.

Two things will help you memorise the bass line:

- The shape, and
- The fingering.

The shape of the bass line

It's helpful to see the bass line as four pairs of notes. In music, pairs of notes are called 'intervals'. An interval is a musical measure of distance. In intervals all the note names are counted.

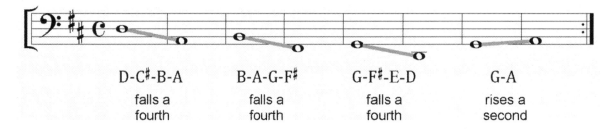

Three pairs are the same, and one is different. The three pairs that are the same 'fall a fourth'; the last pair 'rises a second'.

Look at what happens between the pairs:

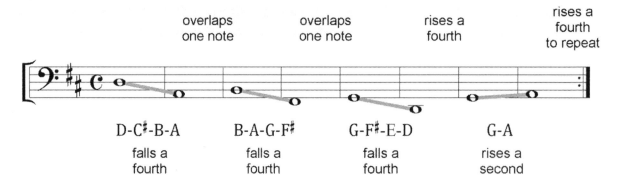

The pairs of fourths overlap by only one scale-tone – 'a second'. From the last note, the bass line rises a fourth to repeat.

As a zig-zag line, the bass line looks like this:

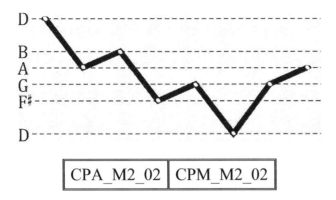

| CPA_M2_02 | CPM_M2_02 |

Practice picking out the bass line from the line diagram alone. The notes are shown down the left hand side.

Fingering the bass line

You will find it easier to remember the bass line if you always use the same fingering to play it. Here is one recommended fingering:

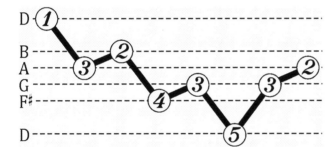

Learning a set fingering will also help you play the bass line from memory. Here's another possibility:

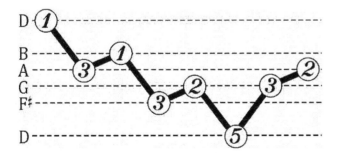

You don't have to use this fingering, but you don't want to run out of fingers on the way down to the low D, or on the way back up.

Experiment, and choose a fingering that suits your hand. Learn the bass line by heart with the fingering of your choice. There is an added advantage to learning the bass line thoroughly; later on, the bass line will teach you the chord sequence as well.

Revise the thirds

Revise the thirds from Module Two, using two hands..

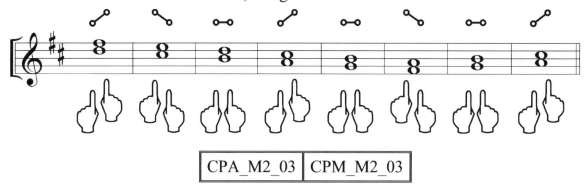

In order to play hands together, you have to be able to play the thirds with the right hand alone. First, play all the thirds with right hand fingers 4 and 2 (RH4 and RH2). – over your backing track recording, if you wish. The left hand does nothing.

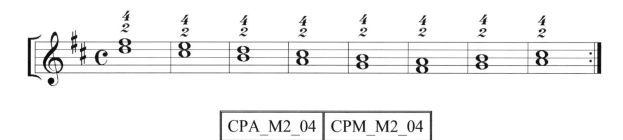

It helps to remember the 'slant' of the thirds – see the lines above the music in the previous example.

To play the thirds more 'joined up' (*legato*), we have to think about the fingering. The simplest thing is to finger the thirds in pairs – 4-2 then 3-1:

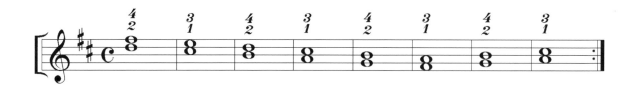

Play well up, towards the back of the keys. You can hear that the fingering makes the pairs sound smoother. (This might not be the final fingering. It may change again as you practice more.)

Put the hands together

Now to put the hands together. Here is the music for the simplest possible version – whole notes in both hands.

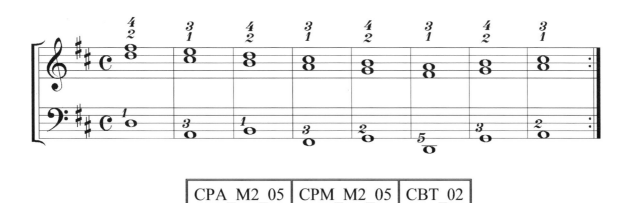

| CPA_M2_05 | CPM_M2_05 | CBT_02 |

Here is your performance over a backing track. Play along, and take over the 'solo'.

| CPA_M2_06 |

Thirds variations in the right hand

An easy way to develop this performance is to 'waggle' the right hand thirds and double the number of left hand notes (making them half-notes/minims). Study the right hand fingering – it helps you not to run out of fingers.

| CPA_M2_07 | CPM_M2_07 |

Next, add the 'next-door-note' feature to the right hand. The right hand fingering again follows a predictable pattern, helping to keep fingers coming.

| CPA_M2_08 | CPM_M2_08 |

The bass line is shown as simple whole notes, but you can play two half-notes per bar if you wish. Finger the bass line sensibly.

Finally, put the third back together on the first beat.

| CPA_M2_09 | CPM_M2_09 |

Practice the right hand on its own first. Notice the 'tweak' in bar 8 – thirds climbing back up to the starting position.

Here are some more Module Two-type patterns written out for the right hand solo:

| CPA_M2_10 | CPM_M2_10 |

The right hand thumb (RH1) note is shown stems-down. The audio and MIDI performance files have a left hand broken chord accompaniment which you will learn in a later module. Play just the roots for now.

The next pattern uses exactly the same notes, but changes the rhythm:

| CPA_M2_11 | CPM_M2_11 |

Only the right hand is given. Supply a left hand.

Again, the right hand fingering – swapping from RH3 to RH2 –keeps making fingers available for the sideways movement of the hand. After bar six, the fingering reverses, to 'creep' the hand the other way

Notice the indication 'sim.' in bar four. 'Sim.' is short for *simile*, which is Italian for 'the same'. It means, carry on fingering the bars in the same way.

Experiment with combining elements of the patterns you have so far:

| CPA_M2_12 | CPM_M2_12 |

Your module audio challenge

Here are two audio-only variations for you to copy.

| CPA_M2_13 |

The second audio-only example changes the rhythm of the bass notes:

| CPA_M2_14 |

The written-out music is in the 'Answers' section at the end of the book.

Practice the patterns until you can play along with the audio or MIDI performance files or over a backing track, then try playing up to speed over a commercial recording.

> **Study tip** If you feel you're getting overwhelmed, go back a step or two to a version you can play successfully. Play that a few times and take a break – it's encouraging to 'quit while you're ahead'!

TRIADS IN THE TREBLE

In Module Three of the Musicarta Canon Project you add a third note to the right hand thirds to make triads (three-note chords) in the treble. Here is a sample audio performance, showing what can be done with the triads you will learn.

> CPA_M3_01

Forming the triads

Listen to the high piano notes in this audio clip:

> CPA_M3_02 | CPM_M3_02

It's the line of thirds in the treble from Modules One and Two.

> CPA_M3_03 | CPM_M3_03

Now listen to the treble notes in this audio clip. They are slightly different.

> CPA_M3_04 | CPM_M3_04

The sound is 'filled out'. A third note has been added below the thirds.

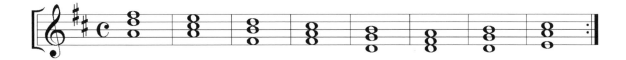

The third note in the treble chords is what we add to the Canon performance in this module.

Playing the triads with two hands

The easiest way to play the triads is to play the new note with the left hand and the thirds with the right.

Revise the thirds, playing with the right hand only. Use any fingering for now.

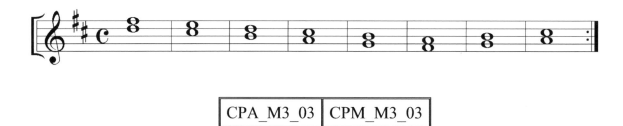

| CPA_M3_03 | CPM_M3_03 |

Here is the new 'voice' (line of notes). Practice with the left hand, using the fingering shown.

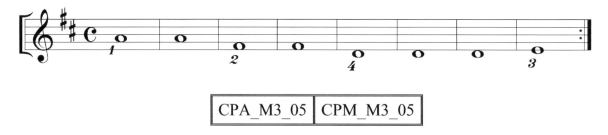

| CPA_M3_05 | CPM_M3_05 |

You need to know this line of notes by heart!

Play the hands together. This music shows the notes on two treble clef staves, right hand on the top, left hand underneath. This makes it obvious which hand plays what. The hands are still right next to each other on the keyboard.

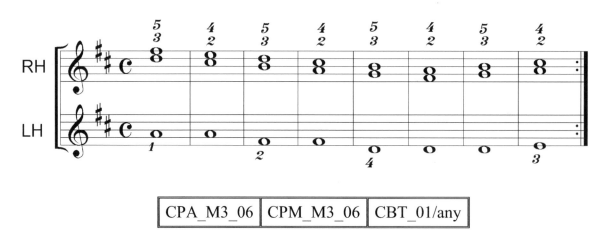

| CPA_M3_06 | CPM_M3_06 | CBT_01/any |

Triad patterns using two hands

You can start playing variations right away by 'waggling' the triads as you did the thirds in Module One. Your part is shown on the (upper) treble clef stave of the following music, with the RH notes stems up, LH notes stems down. Listen to the audio performance files (with chord accompaniment) and study the music of the following examples. Watch the MIDI performance on MidiPiano for more clarity. Play along with a backing track recordings, or with a friend playing the accompaniment.

CPA_M3_07 | CPM_M3_07

CPA_M3_08 | CPM_M3_08

For another variation, you can simply alternate left and right hands twice as quickly.

| CPA_M3_09 | CPM_M3_09 |

Splitting the notes differently

The variations so far have split the three notes of the triad two notes with the right hand and one with the left. You can divide them the other way as well, like this:

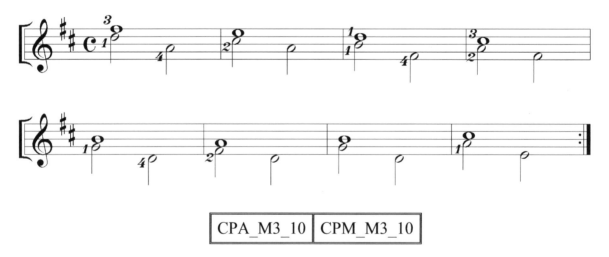

| CPA_M3_10 | CPM_M3_10 |

This makes it much easier to play extra notes in the top voice (line of notes).

CPA_M3_11 | CPM_M3_11

Double the left hand changing speed and use a 'next door note' pattern from the previous modules in the right hand.

CPA_M3_12 | CPM_M3_12

In the following example, you play a top-voice pattern from Module Two over the double-speed left hand notes. In the music, though, the left hand notes are shown as whole notes. In the last four bars, only the basic triads are shown.

Listen to the practice tempo audio file and copy the performance. Fill the full eight bars with the same pattern. Leave out the 'tweaks' in bars seven and eight, if you want to.

Build up to performance tempo and play over your backing track or recording. The audio is up to speed; the MIDI file, which you can study on MidiPiano and play as audio, is at practice speed.

| CPA_M3_13 | CPM_M3_13 |

Musicarta is committed to helping you cultivate a habit of 'messing around with chords', so that whenever you see a triad, your fingers will automatically start bringing it to life with a rhythmic waggle (for example), or an exploration of what the next door notes can add to the performance – the basis of successful pop keyboard technique.

Audio challenge

Listen to this audio performance clip:

| CPA_M3_14 | CPM_M3_14 |

It's a two-bar pattern, nearly the same as the previous, but some notes are missed out in both hands. The left hand doesn't play all its notes in the first bar; the right hand doesn't play all its notes in the second bar. (Look out for the 'tweak' in the last two bars!)

Listen carefully and try to play the pattern. Remember, you can use your media player controls to listen to the clip over and over, and slow it down. The written-out music and the (practice-speed) MIDI file reference number are in the 'Answers' section, if you want to double-check, but at this stage, being prepared to 'have a go' is much more important than getting it absolutely right.

You may also find that, in the course of trying, you come up with a very pleasing version that you actually prefer!

The module performance

The module performance 'mixes and matches' the various keyboard textures you have learned in this module. Listen to it again and see if you can play it by ear. The right hand cell in the table below gives the MIDI file reference number, so you can copy any parts you cannot get by ear from the MidiPiano performance.

CPA_M3_01	CPM_M3_01

Study tip If you double-click on one of the MIDI files in your Canon Project MIDI file folder, Windows Media Player (WMP) will automatically play it as an audio file.

You can set WMP to automatically repeat a track by pressing Ctrl+T, checking 'Repeat' in the Play menu or using the arrowed circle on the control bar. MidiPiano also has an auto-repeat button. Either of these applications will give you a basic, hassle-free play-along track.

You can also slow down a performance in MidiPiano using the 'Speed' slider, and in WMP via 'View'>'Enhancements'>'Play speed settings'.

VOICE MOVEMENT DIAGRAMS

> Study this Supplement as you learn the triad patterns in Modules Three and Four. Come back regularly to refresh your memory, and make voice movement diagrams a part of your creative keyboard thinking.

Voice movement diagrams

Voice movement diagrams (VMDs) make it a lot easier to learn and remember strings of triads that move about a lot – like the top parts of the Canon. In particular, it's useful to look for patterns in how the three individual chord 'voices' (notes) move.

We say 'voices' because we are imagining that the triad is sung by a three-voice choir. Between chords, a voice usually moves to the closest note – it doesn't jump around.

In the Canon, our two original treble (right hand) voices 'sing' the thirds – one the upper, the other the lower note..

| CPA_VMD_01 | CPM_VMD_01 |

The lines show how the voices move. You see that they move in parallel, always a third apart. Play the thirds with the right hand.

The new voice sings the bottom note of the triad.

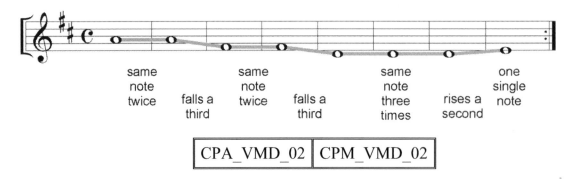

| CPA_VMD_02 | CPM_VMD_02 |

You see that the new voice 'sings' two notes the same, then another pair of notes, then three notes the same and lastly one on its own. You need to know this line by heart. Practice the left hand, using any convenient fingering.

The chords in pairs

Adding the two lines together, we get this:

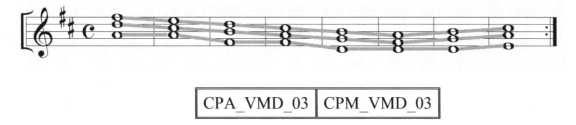

| CPA_VMD_03 | CPM_VMD_03 |

Thinking of the chords in pairs, as we did with the bass line, is much more useful:

| CPA_VMD_04 | CPM_VMD_04 |

If we exaggerate the shapes, we get these useful 'voice movement diagrams'.

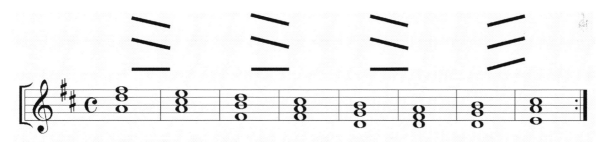

Listen to the last audio clip a few times and imagine you can 'hear' the VMD shapes.

Looking, you can see three 'movements' that are obviously the same, and one that's different – just like the bass line.

The voice movement diagrams (VMDs) say:

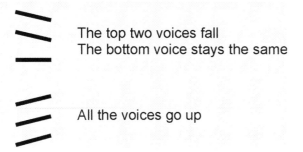

The top two voices fall
The bottom voice stays the same

All the voices go up

You only have to remember the bottom notes, and the voice movement diagrams give you virtually the full 'recipe' for the chords. (You also have to remember the fourth, greyed-out, VMD.)

31

Study the VMDs together with the chords they apply to. This is the most efficient way of memorizing a string of chords.

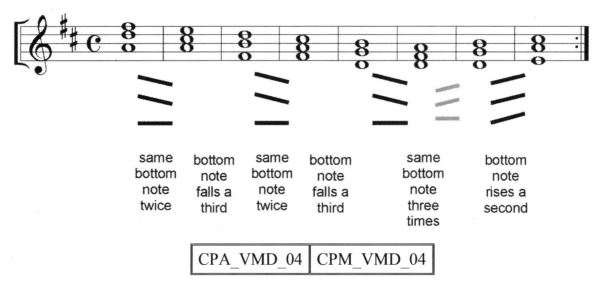

same bottom note twice	bottom note falls a third	same bottom note twice	bottom note falls a third	same bottom note three times	bottom note rises a second

CPA_VMD_04	CPM_VMD_04

As a popular music keyboard player, you will use triads in the right hand all the time, and VMDs are a great help for seeing in your mind's eye (and remembering) what the notes in the chords are doing.

Voice movement diagram chart

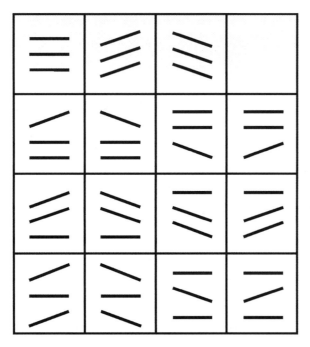

Here is the complete set of voice movement diagrams.

Lots of popular music is based on chord changes you can remember using VMDs.

Try using the idea behind VMDs to generate your own compositions and in your own music 'shorthand' (either written or just 'thought').

Note that VMDs only indicate how the 'voices' more relative to each other, and not how far apart the notes of a chord are or how far the move.

Preferably, chord voices will move to next door scale tones.

TRIADS IN THE RIGHT HAND

To take your Canon performance any further, you have to be able to play the Canon piano chords with the right hand alone. This is a simple matter of fingering. From these right hand triads, you can then make beautiful-sounding broken chord patterns – the heart of modern popular keyboard playing.

Here is a sample of what you will learn to play in this module.

CPA_M4_01

Fingering the Canon right hand triads

We move forward with the Canon Project by playing the Module Three triads with the right hand alone. The right hand Canon chords are fingered in four pairs.

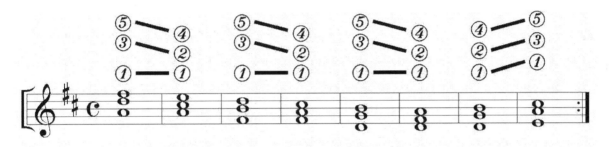

CPA_M4_02   CPM_M4_02

You see that a 'next-door note, next-door finger' principle applies. Fingers 5 and 3 always fall to 4 and 2, with the opposite in the last pair. The thumb always plays the bottom note.

Revise the bass line

As your performances get more complicated, it's essential to have at least one hand that comes 'practically automatically'. Revise the bass line from the familiar diagrams below, paying particular attention to the fingering, which is the secret of this dependability.

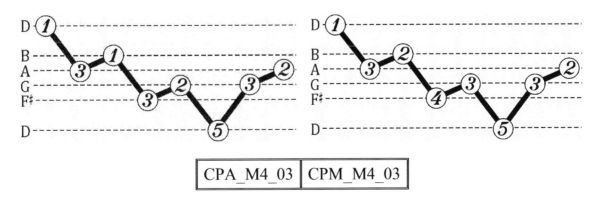

CPA_M4_03   CPM_M4_03

Right hand triads and bass line together

Play the right hand triads plus the bass line. Try to finger them correctly from the start. Play them on their own first, then over one of your backing tracks.

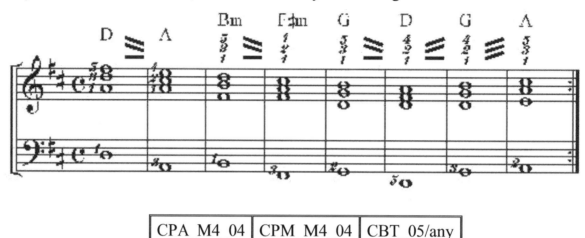

| CPA_M4_04 | CPM_M4_04 | CBT_05/any |

Notice the voice movement diagrams (VMDs) between the chords. Use them to help you remember how the chord tones move. (The letters above the chords are chord symbols. You learn about chord symbols in the next module.)

Solo right hand triad patterns

See if you can play these triad patterns from previous Canon Project modules with the right hand alone, over your left hand single-note bass line.

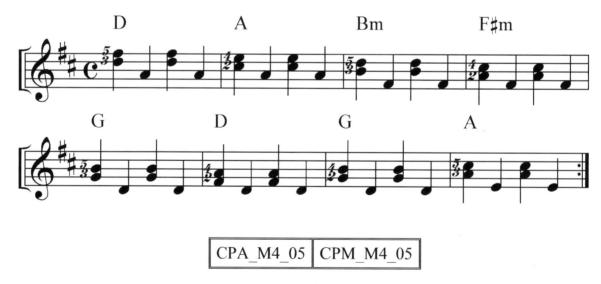

| CPA_M4_05 | CPM_M4_05 |

Note that all the music – stems-up or stems-down – is now right hand music.

You only need to change the length of some notes or chords to get quite a different feel. Listen to the next performance audio.

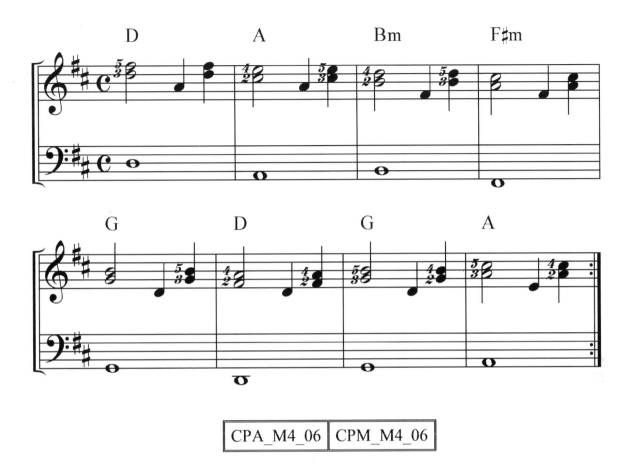

| CPA_M4_06 | CPM_M4_06 |

Develop the bass line

Take advantage of the relatively simple right hand chord pattern to develop the bass line. Listen to what the bass does in the next audio performance file. It plays two notes per bar. Both notes are roots – the name note of the chord – but an octave apart, and the bass 'bounces' between them. Just listen , for now.

| CPA_M4_07 | CPM_M4_07 | CBT_D01 |

When you get a new 'trick' like this to master, it's a good idea to simplify things if you can, and build up to the new thing gently. For example, it would be a good idea to study and practice the new 'bouncing' bass line on its own, first:

| CPA_M4_08 | CPM_M4_08 |

Then rehearse the new bass with plain chords:

| CPA_M4_09 | CPX_M4_09 |

Only then should you 'put it all together'. Build-ups .like these take a little longer and can feel like a waste of time, but they're far better than trying and trying and getting discouraged. Build-ups also encourage you to see performance as a combination of elements, which is the creative way to see music.

Here is the written-out music for the 'bouncing bass' performance. Don't let yourself be hypnotised by the leger lines in the bass clef. The chord symbol (the letter above the music) tells you what both the bass notes are – you don't have to count down the lines to find out.

CPA_M4_10

It doesn't matter if you don't play the bass line exactly as written – just play two root notes per bar with the left hand. You might prefer a different top root/bottom root pattern. Also, you can play the whole left hand part an octave higher – especially if you're working on a shorter electronic keyboard.

Play the chords an octave lower

Finally, find the right hand chords an octave lower. The chords will be written in the bass clef, using leger lines (which you may find confusing), but the chord shapes and note names are the same, just an octave lower. So find and play the chords first, then check the music to see what they look like.

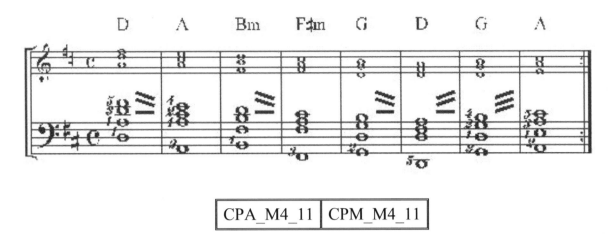

| CPA_M4_11 | CPM_M4_11 |

Find the chords in the new place and rehearse them a few times. Use any of the drum backing tracks (CBT_D…) and see if they inspire some rhythm in your performance.

Audio challenge

Now, listen to this audio clip. It's the chords you've just found played with a slow rock ballad feel. The left hand plays two bass notes per bar, on beats one and four.

| CPA_M4_12 | CBT_D01 |

Try to play this variation by ear from the audio clip. Note the recommended drum backing track. The written-out music and the MIDI file reference number are in the 'Answers' section of the book.

Study Tip Support file reference numbers

The numbers in the support file tables are coded as follows:

CPA Canon Project Audio – the MP3 audio file for the example.

CPM Canon Project MIDI – the MIDI file. Play in MidiPiano to see-and-hear or in your media player as basic-quality audio, or load into your sequencer to experiment with.

CBT Canon Backing Track – an audio backing track. Play and loop in Audacity (preferably) or your regular media player.

CBT_D… Canon Backing Track_Drums. An audio drum backing track. Short, and best looped in Audacity.

BROKEN CHORD PATTERNS

Music often breaks up triads and plays the three notes one after another in regular, repeating, 'broken chord' patterns. For the keyboard player, broken chord patterns offer a great way of getting more 'mileage' out of knowing a chord.

CPA_M5_01

If we call the three notes of a triad bottom (B), middle (M) and top (T), we can use a BMT shorthand to notate broken patterns, getting away from the notes and making the patterns easier to understand and remember.

Broken chord patterns

Here is an example of a broken chord pattern with the BMT 'coding' written in.

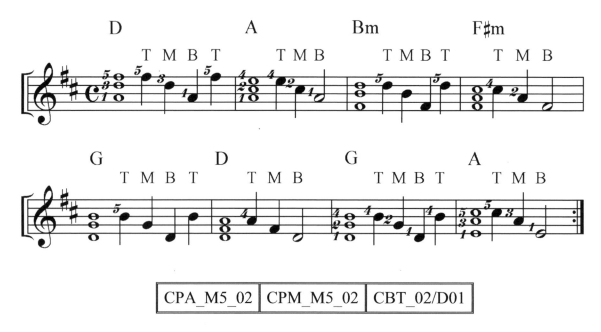

CPA_M5_02 | CPM_M5_02 | CBT_02/D01

You don't play the whole note chords at the start of the bar – they are just there so that:

- You can see that the chords are the same triads you just learned in Module Four, and
- You can see how the BMT coding describes the broken chord pattern.

The BMT coding for this pattern is:

‖: T M B T | T M B :‖

Practice the pattern until you can play it comfortably. Use the MIDI performance as a visual aid in MidiPiano if necessary.

Bottom, middle, top (BMT) coding as musical shorthand

Here is a 'BMT shorthand' sketch which shows exactly the same music as the previous example.

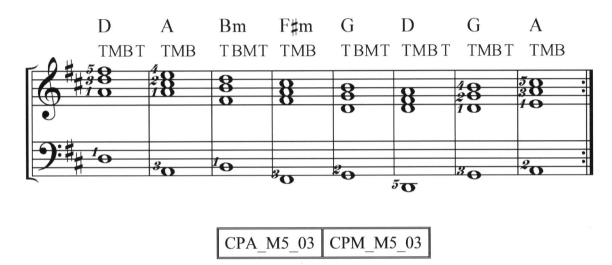

| CPA_M5_03 | CPM_M5_03 |

Try to play the broken chord pattern, with a bass line, from just the BMT sketch.

A BMT challenge

Here is another broken chord pattern for you to play.

| CPA_M5_04 | CPM_M5_04 |

The rhythm and the chords are just the same, but the order of notes is slightly different. The BMT coding for this pattern is:

‖T B M T |T M B :‖

Try to play the pattern right the way through the chord sequence using just the audio and the BMT coding. Watch the MidiPiano performance for more visual learning. The actual music – in the 'Answers' section – shows a mixture of chords, notes and pure BMT shorthand.

Continuous right hand broken chord patterns

The broken chord patterns above give you time move your hand to the new fingering group – the next pair of chords. To play continuous broken chord patterns, you have to adjust the fingering slightly to 'keep the fingers coming' (like a caterpillar track), so your hand can creep continuously across the keyboard.

CPA_M5_05	CPM_M5_05

The BMT coding for the pattern above is:

$$\|: T \quad M \quad B \quad T \quad | \quad T \quad M \quad B \quad T \quad :\|$$

Play the Canon chord sequence right through using the broken chord pattern given.

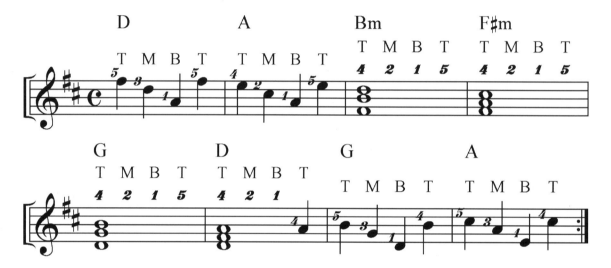

The BMT coding for the next pattern is:

$$\|: T \quad B \quad M \quad T \quad | \quad T \quad B \quad M \quad T \quad :\|$$

… so the fingering has to be slightly different.

Try to play the whole chorus (8 bars) from just the BMT sketch:

| CPA_M5_06 | CPM_M5_06 |

Take time out to enjoy your accomplishment. Rehearse all the patterns, experiment and get comfortable with your broken chords before going on to the next section.

Audio challenge

Combine the Module Four thirds with a broken chord texture. Use the last BMT pattern again but play thirds where it says 'T' instead of a single top note. Play the pattern over the 'bouncing' bass line from Module Four.

‖:T B M T │T B M T :‖

| CPA_M5_07 | CPM_M5_07 |

Try to work just from the instructions and the audio first. Remember the Module Four advice about 'build-ups' – practice over a simple bass line first. Use MidiPiano for a visual demonstration if you need to. The written-out music is in the 'Answers' section.

Go digital!

Go digital! Even as a novice, you can easily make backing tracks from commercial Canon recordings using 'Audacity', a free, easy-to-use sound editor. Download and install, then Google "Editing audio in Audacity" and follow the instructions from any of the web pages on offer.

If you don't want to have Audacity running as you play, you can make and save longer backing tracks (in Audacity) with a simple copy-and-paste operation, just like in a word processor. If you want to save your tracks as MP3 files, you will need an additional MP3 encoder. You can read it all up on the Audacity site.

Audacity also offers more accurate 'looping' than Windows Media Player's 'repeat' function. If you don't need to trim your sound clip, shift+spacebar automatically turns Audacity's 'loop' feature on. If you do need to trim, the internet offers plenty of Audacity tutorial material.

You will find your Canon Project backing tracks (designated CBT_...) in the Canon Backing Tracks folder. Your Musicarta Canon Project backing tracks are cut off exactly at chorus-end, so whether looping or extending, your backing track will always stay in time.

Audacity and MidiPiano provide an excellent introduction to digital audio, with all its potential in learning situations. Once you have mastered the essentials, you will easily think of many applications – and classical teachers especially will benefit with their pupils from demonstrating a bit of digital know-how!

THE CANON CHORD SEQUENCE

To get anywhere in popular music, you must be able to understand and use chord symbols. Chord symbols tell you which notes – mainly the chord tones – will sound good at a particular point in the music. Chord tones (mainly) and 'next-door' scale tones are then used in the melody and for soloing and improvisation.

This module also introduces 'inversions'. The simplest chord is made of three notes – the chord tones – and any one of the three notes can be at the top. You have to understand this, in practical terms, to move forward in your playing.

Here is a broken-chord inversions study based on the content of this module.

| CPA_M6_01 | CPM_M6_01 |

Study tip There is a lot of new information in this module. It is not necessary to understand it all perfectly in order to carry on working through the Musicarta Canon Project, but, if you aim to 'just sit down and play', you will, in the end, want to know this material 'in your bones'.

Also, in order to find the chord tones – essential for interpreting chord symbols – you need to know your D major scale. Use the scale practice patterns in the Key of D Major supplement at the end of the book, and start all your Canon Project sessions with some D major scale work.

The Canon chord symbols

Here is the music example we will be working with.

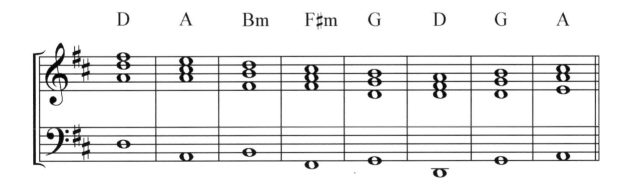

| CPA_M6_02 | CPM_M6_02 |

Notice that the letter in the chord symbol also names the bass (left hand) note. In popular music, the bass note is usually the name-note (root) of the chord.

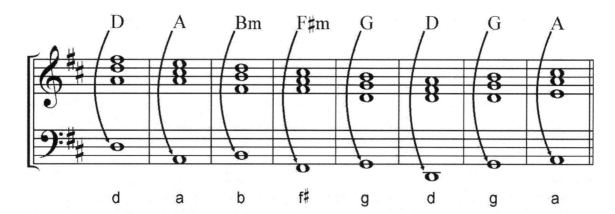

Inversions

Now look at the chords in the treble clef. You see that two chord symbols – D and A – have two different chord shapes under them.

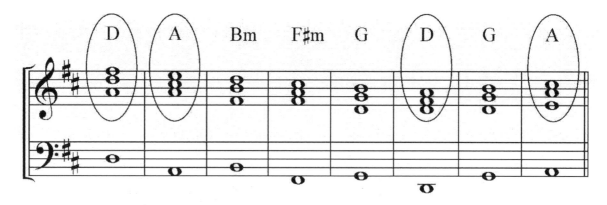

How can these different shapes be the same chord? Because they are inversions – the two chords are made up of the same notes.

Look at the D chords illustration on next page. The D and F sharp notes can be either side of the A. Copy the audio and MIDI performance clips to discover the inversions.

| CPA_M6_03 | CPM_M6_03 |

Do the same thing with the two A chords (following page). Here, only one note (E) moves from bottom to top, but both chords are made from A, C sharp and E notes.

| CPA_M6_04 | CPM_M6_04 |

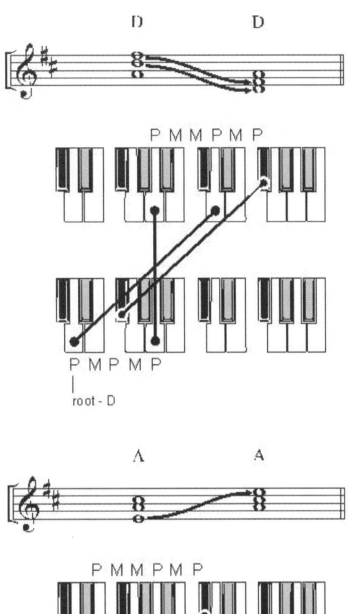

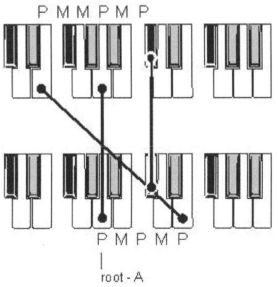

45

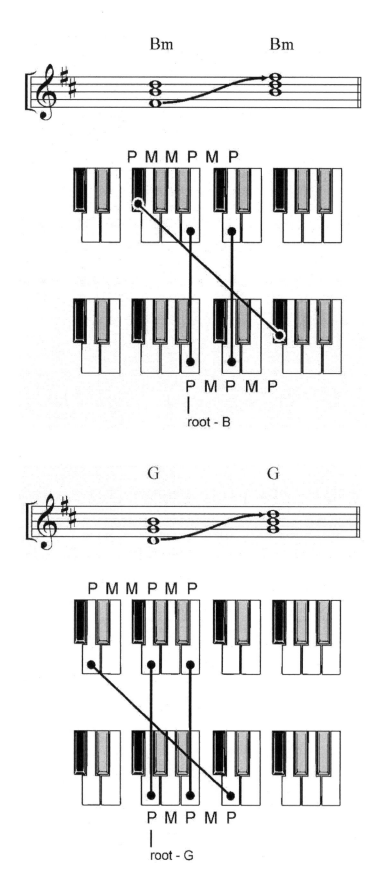

'Root position triads' – PMPMP chords

Note the 'P' and 'M' in the keyboard illustrations. They stand for 'play one' and 'miss one' (D major scale tones). Once chords are flipped into 'play one, miss one, play one, miss one , play one' arrangement (PMPMP), they are called 'root position triads', and only then can we name them after the lowest note.

Flip the B minor and G chords into root position (illustrations on previous page). The audio clips are arranged B minor first, then G.

CPA_M6_05	CPM_M6_05

CPA_M6_06	CPM_M6_06

The roots in the Canon RH triads

Here are all the Canon chords again, with the roots of the right hand triads indicated.

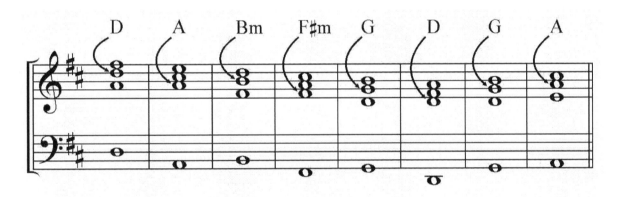

CPA_M6_07	CPM_M6_07

Copy the audio/MIDI performance. It's essential that you start to 'see' the root of the right hand chords, which is often not the bottom note.

Forming inversions

Inversions are named upwards from root position. You make the first inversion by taking the bottom note of a root position triad up an octave to the top. Repeating the operation gives you the second inversion. The third time you perform the operation, you get back to a root position (PMPMP) triad.

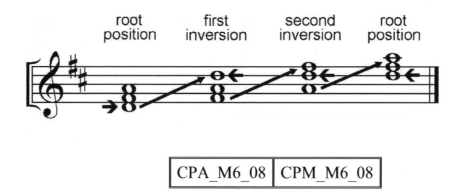

| CPA_M6_08 | CPM_M6_08 |

(These are all D chords. The arrowed note is the root, or name-note.)

You can just as easily make inversions by taking the top note to the bottom, but then the counting goes 'the wrong way' – root position, second inversion, first inversion, root position.

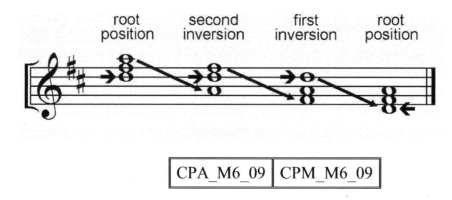

| CPA_M6_09 | CPM_M6_09 |

Practising inverting the Canon chords

Practising making inversions, and cycling through them, helps you see the chords in the keyboard, and is essential work for any modern keyboard player. Also, broken chord studies, which cycle through the inversions, are practically ready-made music.

Here is the inversion drill in D.

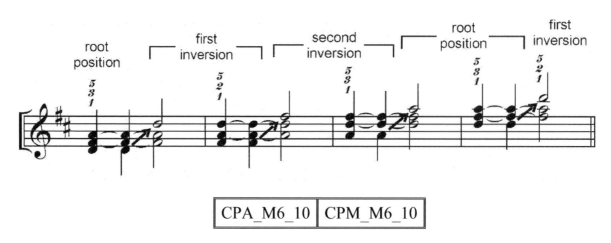

| CPA_M6_10 | CPM_M6_10 |

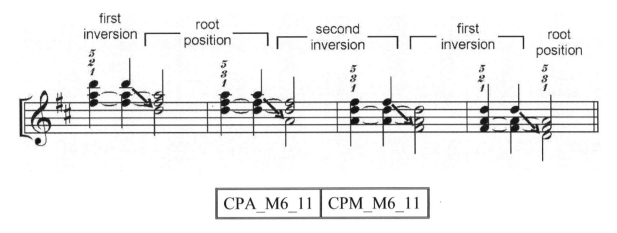

| first inversion | root position | second inversion | first inversion | root position |

| CPA_M6_11 | CPM_M6_11 |

Practice until you understand the pattern, then perform this inversion drill for all five Canon chords. Here are your starting chords shown on keyboards, and what your practice should sound like.

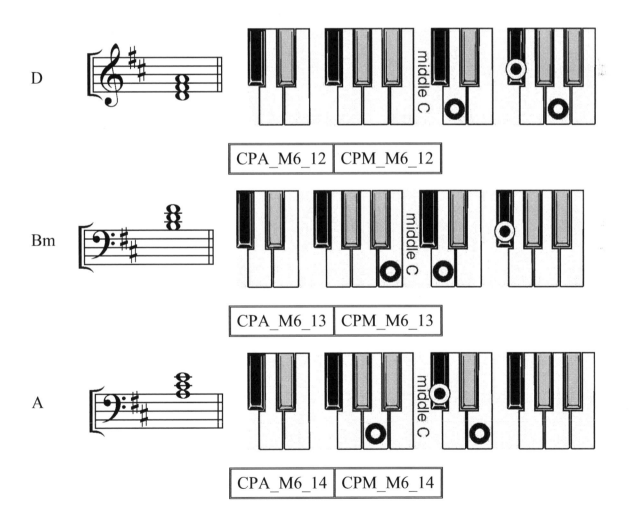

D

| CPA_M6_12 | CPM_M6_12 |

Bm

| CPA_M6_13 | CPM_M6_13 |

A

| CPA_M6_14 | CPM_M6_14 |

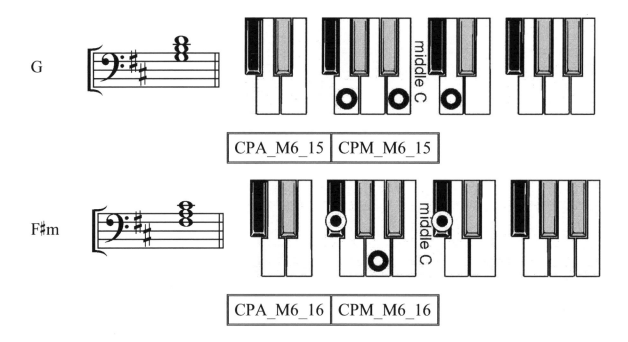

G

CPA_M6_15 | CPM_M6_15

F#m

CPA_M6_16 | CPM_M6_16

Broken chord studies

Cycling speedily through the inversions of a chord gives what are called broken chord studies. All the major exam syllabuses include broken chord studies.

The simplest broken chord study (in D) is this:

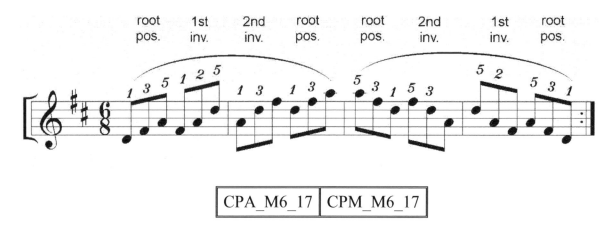

CPA_M6_17 | CPM_M6_17

The pattern plays broken-up root position, first inversion, second inversion and root positions rising, and reverses the order of the notes and chords to come back down. This is the broken chord pattern used in the module performance.

Notice the fingering. This is the 'official' fingering for inversions – fingers 1, 3, 5 for the root position and second inversion, and 1, 2, 5 for the first inversion. This is how the inversions best fit the hand – you should try to adopt it as your standard fingering. The temptation is never to use the second finger.

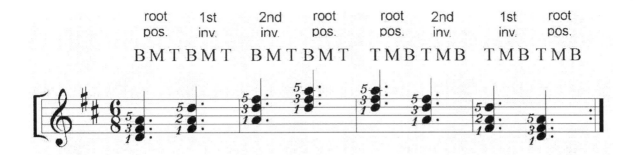

Make sure you understand the pattern by comparing this diagrams with the written-out pattern above, and then play it on all five Canon chords, starting on the root poeition triads you used for the inversion drill.

The table gives the pattern in the remaining Canon chords – B minor, A, G and F sharp minor. Remember, you can pause and rewind to keep up, and slow down MIDI playback in MidiPiano.

CPA/M_M6_18	CPA/M_M6_19
CPA/M_M6_20	CPA/M_M6_21

A Canon broken chord study

Earlier in the module, we promised that broken chord study patterns were already 'practically music'. Here's the proof! Listen to this Canon keyboard texture and try to hear what's happening – before you look at the music below.

CPA_M6_22	CPM_M6_22

The right hand climbs up the inversions in D (first of a pair of chords), then slides down the inversions in A (second chord of the pair) from the note arrived at.

The music for the first pair of chord (D – A) is written out, but only the pattern is shown in the second line, which indicates how to 'think' the formula for the music.

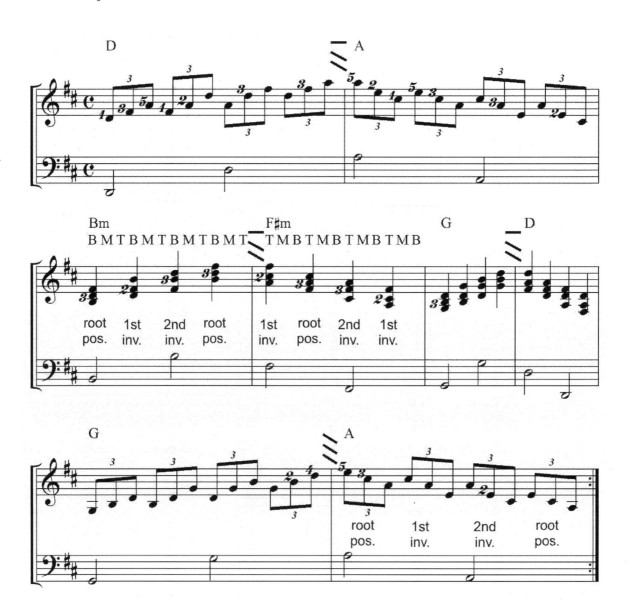

Note the voice movement diagrams at the middle of the pairs, where the chord changes. The top 'voice' stays the same, the bottom two drop. You need to know your D major scale to know which notes they drop to.

Note the fingering. Try at least to remember to use finger 2 in the first inversion chord. You have to deviate from standard fingering to make changing chord easier.

The left hand in the audio performance plays a 'bouncing bass'. You don't have to play exactly as written – any roots will do.

Audio challenge

Here is another Canon broken chord study.

CPA_M6_23	CPM_M6_23

Note: The treble (right hand) does not always move to the next chord tone – it sometimes skips over to the next chord tone but one.

Try to get the pattern and copy the performance. The two-bar pattern repeats; you only have to 'get' the first one to fill up three quarters of the chorus. As usual , the last pair is slightly different.

Here is the Canon chord sequence again, to assist your listening.

:D	A	Bm	F#m	G	D	G	A :

The written-out music, with some notes, is the 'Answers' section.

Hopefully, you will see from this module that regular broken chord practice will repay your efforts. It's a great way to 'doodle' at the keyboard, and broken chord patterns provide an off-the-shelf option for playing a chord sequence. You will find more broken chord patterns to practice on the Musicarta website via the 'Chords' navbar tab.

If you want to learn more chord theory, there is a Major and Minor Chords supplement explaining the difference between major and minor chords (dealing specifically with the Canon chords) at the back of this book.

ACCOMPANIMENT PATTERNS

Most pieces of music have a musical background which supports the melody. This background is not random – it often repeats the notes of the chords in the chord sequence in predictable, rhythmic patterns. The successful modern keyboard player needs to be able to devise these accompaniment patterns from chord symbols.

Here is the module audio performance, which plays some of the treble patterns you've learnt previously over the accompaniment pattern you'll be learning in this module.

CPA_M7_01

Naming the chord tones

Accompaniment patterns are usually made from the root, the third and the fifth (the chord tones) of the chord named in the chord symbol. In the Canon, we find them by counting D major scale tones up from the root (name-note) of the chord, whichever chard it is, as shown in the next illustration. The root is number one – there is no zero in this kind of counting.

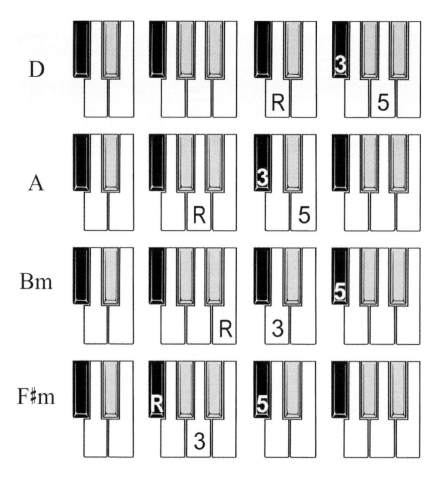

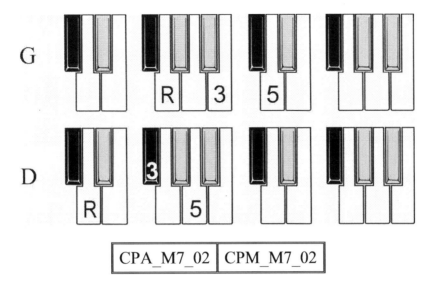

| CPA_M7_02 | CPM_M7_02 |

You have found these notes before, but you didn't name them as chord tones root, third and fifth. Find them again and name the notes as you play them, as in the audio file.

The chord tones keep their own names wherever they are on the keyboard. The note F sharp is always the third of a D major chord, whether it's above or below the D in a chord, and so on.

Here are the chord tones of our five Canon chords, played and named from around the D below middle C.

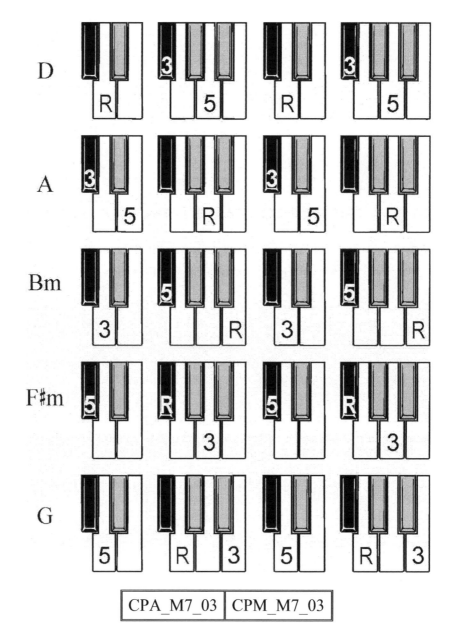

D

A

Bm

F#m

G

| CPA_M7_03 | CPM_M7_03 |

Find and play the notes, saying the chord tone names.

Sometimes, though, it's useful to give the root and the third different names, especially when there are four notes to name – as you'll learn in the next section.

Canon accompaniment patterns

The Canon accompaniment has four strong beats for each chord in the chord sequence. (Listen for them in one of your audio performance tracks.) We can get four notes by playing another root note an octave above the first one. We call this second root note 'the octave' (8), to show it's a different key on the keyboard.

We say we have 'doubled' the root because we play the second note as well as, not instead of, the first.

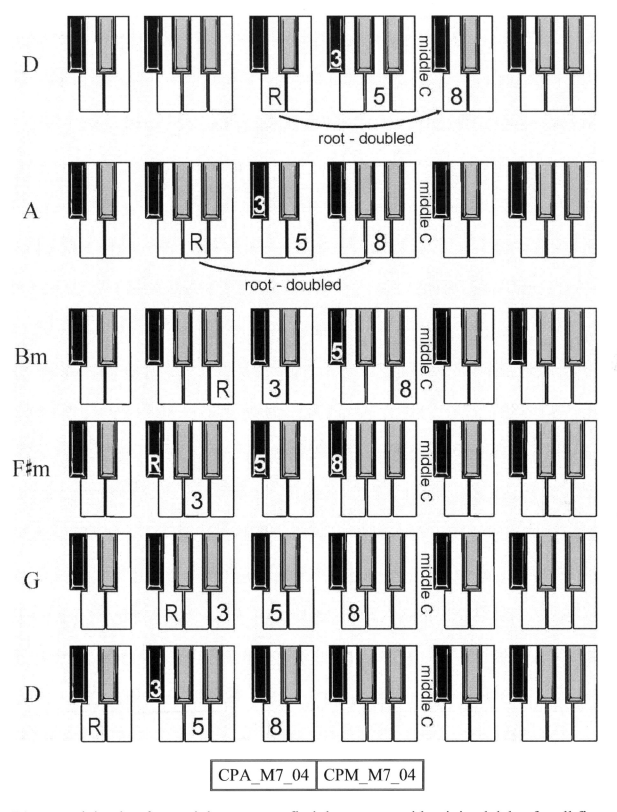

root - doubled

root - doubled

| CPA_M7_04 | CPM_M7_04 |

It's essential going forward that you can find these notes with minimal delay for all five Canon chords. Drill using both hands and be sure to say the chord tone names.

The R, 5, 8, 10 accompaniment pattern

The most attractive four-note chord tone pattern takes the third (3) of the R, 3, 5, 8 pattern up an octave. To show that the third is in a new place, we call it 'the tenth' (10), carrying on counting up from the octave (8).

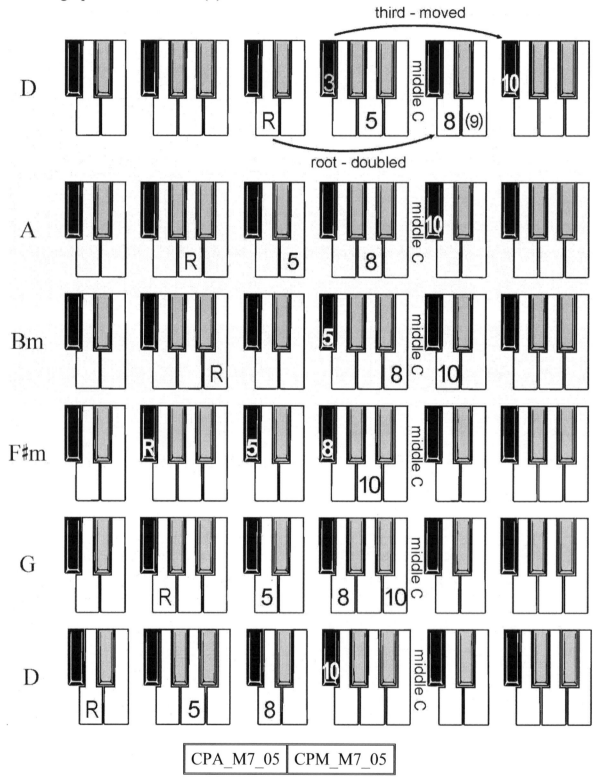

| CPA_M7_05 | CPM_M7_05 |

Note that:

- The tenth (10) is the third (3), but an octave higher. (We call it the tenth to remind us it's above the octave.)
- The octave (8) is the root (R), but an octave higher.

Find the root, fifth, octave and tenth, in that order, of all the chords in the Canon chord sequence. Play the root (R) with the left hand, and the fifth (5), octave (8) and tenth (10) with the right hand.

Practicing the R, 5, 8, 10 accompaniment pattern

We will be using this accompaniment a lot in the Canon Project, so you need to know it well. Practice playing the pattern L, R, R, R until you can play along with this practice-speed audio track.

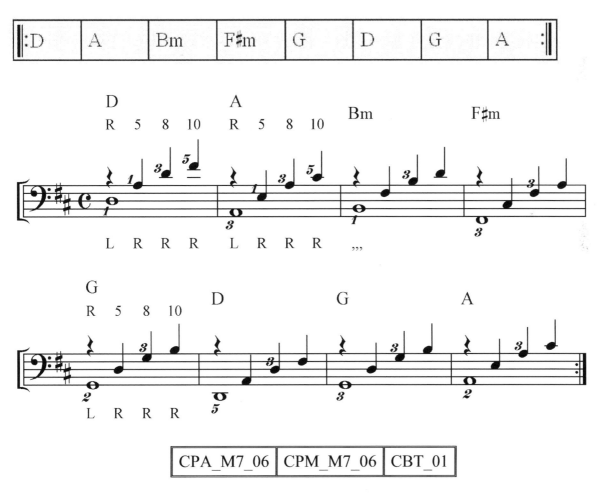

| CPA_M7_06 | CPM_M7_06 | CBT_01 |

There is a lot of information in the illustration above. Reading from the top, you see the chord symbol (D, A etc.), then the chord tone order R, 3, 5, 8. Then comes the actual music, with fingering, and lastly the reminder to play the notes one with the left hand and three with the right (L, R, R, R).

Finding the notes is your first priority, but you should also be trying to use proper/bass line fingering. Here is the bass line with the fingering given in the music above:

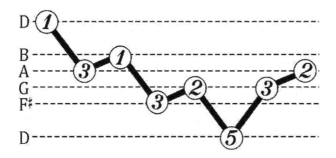

You can use your own preferred fingering if you wish, but always start on LH1 on the top D and get down to LH5 for the bottom D and back up without running out of fingers.

In this accompaniment pattern, the right hand always uses fingers 1, 3, 5. If you make the octave (8) your 'target note' when you move to a new chord and always put your right hand third finger (RH3) over it, your right hand thumb (RH1) and little finger (RH5) will be in the right place almost automatically. Here's a little exercise to make that clearer.

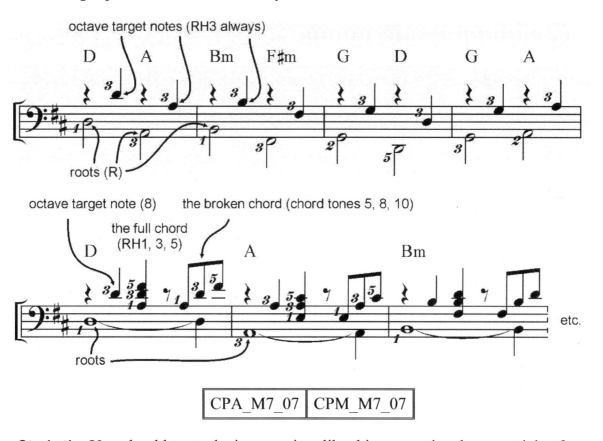

| CPA_M7_07 | CPM_M7_07 |

Study tip You should try to devise exercises like this to practice the essentials of whatever you're learning. You try to establish what you absolutely have to do for things to go right, or what you're not sure about, or where you go wrong, and practice just exactly that. This is much more economical and encouraging than just 'hacking through' on a trial-and-error basis again and again!

Playing the accompaniment pattern different ways

One really good way to get to know the notes of the accompaniment pattern is to split them up between the hands in different ways.

Run through the chord sequence using these three different combinations.

1. **Type One**: Play the root with the left hand and the other three notes with the right (L, R, R, R)

2. **Type Two**: Play the root and the fifth with the left hand, and the octave and tenth with the right (L, L, R, R)

3. **Type Three**: Play three notes with the left hand and just one with the right (L, L, L, R)

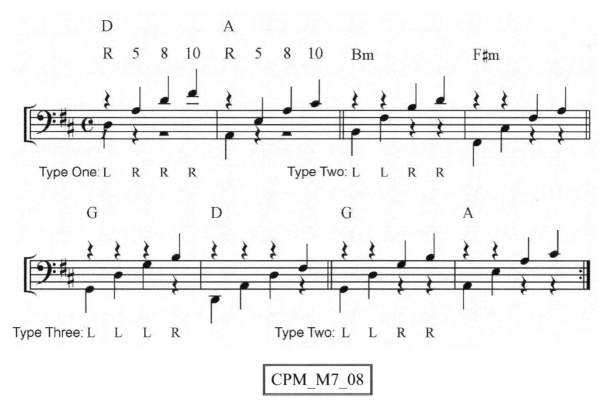

CPM_M7_08

Two bars of each type are shown in the music, but you should play whole choruses (8 bars) of each type, as demonstrated in the MIDI performance file.

This exercise might seem like 'just extra work', but experience shows it is very effective preparation for playing the accompaniment with the left hand alone. For clarity, the notes are all shown as one-beat crotchets, but you should try to make your fingers 'sticky' and layer the notes up to make a four-note stack by the end of each bar. You will see this in the MIDI performance on MidiPiano.

61

Enjoy your accomplishment! Play R, 5, 8, 10 patterns through the entire chord sequence in time with a backing track or up-to-speed classical Canon recordings or YouTube performances.

CPA_M7_09

The chord sequence repeats, so you can easily join in again if you lose your place.

Playing duets with this accompaniment

If you know somebody else who is also working through the Musicarta Canon Project, or are working through the project with a teacher, you can play the Canon as a duet.

In duets, the treble (top) part is called the 'primo', and the bass accompaniment is called the 'secondo' One person ('primo') can play any of the patterns from the previous Canon Project modules with two hands in the treble, while the other person ('secondo') plays the accompaniment pattern in the bass – using any combination of left and right hands.

CPA_M7_10	CPM_M7_10	CBT_02

You can download some written-out duet music from the Musicarta site via the Canon tab on the site navbar. The performance recorded above is just a suggestion.

In the download music, the primo part is written on one treble clef stave and the secondo part on the bass clef stave. For both parts, right hand notes are written stems-up and left hand notes, stems down.

For variety, the secondo (accompaniment) player can play different combinations of left hand and right hand notes as drilled in the previous exercise and demonstrated in the MIDI performance file.

The 'primo' player can take the opportunity to showcase any new variations they have discovered in the course of their learning.

ACCOMPANIMENT WITH RIGHT HAND THIRDS

A solo performer needs to be able to play the accompaniment in the left hand while the right hand plays the melody – the music the listener mostly hears. In this module, you will be playing some of the right hand thirds patterns from Modules One and Two over your own left hand solo accompaniment. Here is one of the combinations you will build up to in this module:

CPA_M8_01

It's essential to know the R, 5, 8, 10 left hand accompaniment pattern in all six Canon chord positions by heart to play solo Canon variations. Revise the pattern using the three different left hand/right hand combinations suggested in Module Seven, using this 'practice prompt':

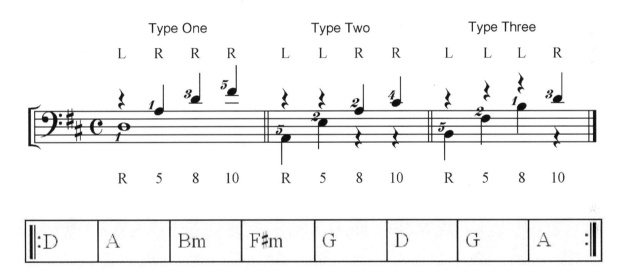

Play through the whole chord sequence using the Type One (L, R, R, R) hand combination, then using Type Two (L, L, R, R), then Type Three (L, L, L, R). Use the MIDI performance file CPM_M7_08 from Module Seven to guide you.

Playing the accompaniment pattern with the left hand

Playing the accompaniment with the left hand alone is made possible by passing the left hand second finger (LH2) over to play the fourth chord tone – the tenth (10). Play the R, 5, 8, 10 pattern through the whole Canon chord sequence using the 5, 2, 1, 2 fingering to start getting the feel of it.

Note that you would never usually have the fingering put in every bar (as in the following music) – that's just a reminder for the first time you do it.

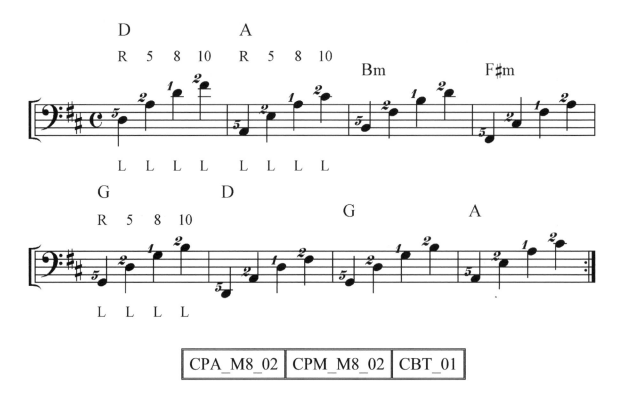

| CPA_M8_02 | CPM_M8_02 | CBT_01 |

Practising the 5, 2, 1, 2 fingering

When you play a solo version of the Canon, the right hand plays the more interesting, more complicated music, so the left hand has to be practically automatic. Only lots of practice makes finding the R, 5, 8, 10 chord tones with the left hand alone, easy.

You will find three pages of left hand accompaniment practice patterns (PP) in the Accompaniment Practice Patterns supplement at the back of this book. Practise each exercise on a number of different chords – use the R, 5, 8, 10 coding to find the right notes.

The table shows the audio and MIDI performance files (CPA/M) for the patterns. The audio and MIDI files for the practice patterns are in the separate CP PP audio + MIDI folder. Remember, you can use MIDI files as basic-quality audio files, too.

CPA/M_M8_PP_1	CPA/M_M8_PP_5	CPA/M_M8_PP_9
CPA/M_M8_PP_2	CPA/M_M8_PP_6	CPA/M_M8_PP_10
CPA/M_M8_PP_3	CPA/M_M8_PP_7	CPA/M_M8_PP_11
CPA/M_M8_PP_4	CPA/M_M8_PP_8	CPA/M_M8_PP_12

Don't be put off by how many practice patterns there are. Do a little practice every day. Most keyboard left hand accompaniment patterns in any music are made from the root, fifth, octave and tenth chord tones, so the practice you put into getting the Canon left hand dependable will pay off with dividends in the future.

Now go back and play the LH solo R, 5, 8, 10 accompaniment again, from just this chord sequence chart.

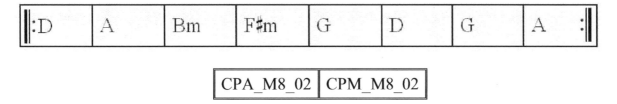

| CPA_M8_02 | CPM_M8_02 |

When you can do this, go on to the next section.

LH accompaniment with RH thirds patterns

You are going to play a solo Canon versions made from the new LH solo bass accompaniment pattern plus the thirds from Module One.

First, you have to make sure you can play the treble (melody) parts with your right hand alone. Here are the plain thirds with the another possible RH solo fingering.

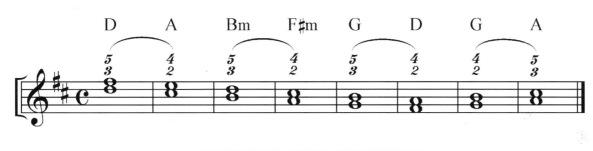

| CPA_M8_03 | CPM_M8_03 |

Notice that the fingering allows the four pairs of thirds to be played legato (as shown by the slurs). Practice the right hand solo at the speed given.

Now play the thirds over the LH solo R, 5, 8, 10 accompaniment 'ladders'.

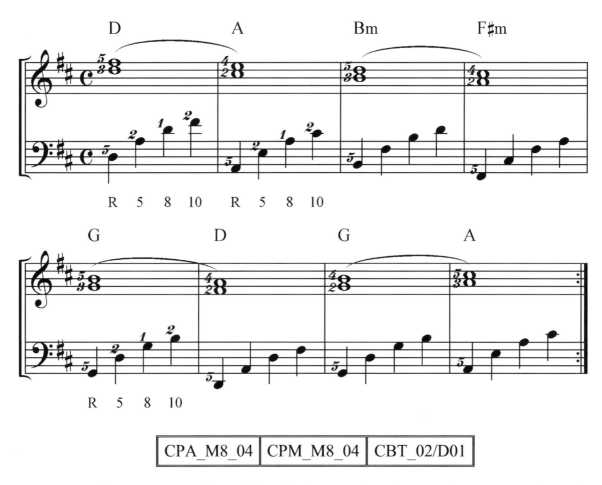

| CPA_M8_04 | CPM_M8_04 | CBT_02/D01 |

You can break up and 'roll' the thirds as before. Notice the new fingering, which helps 'keep the fingers coming'.

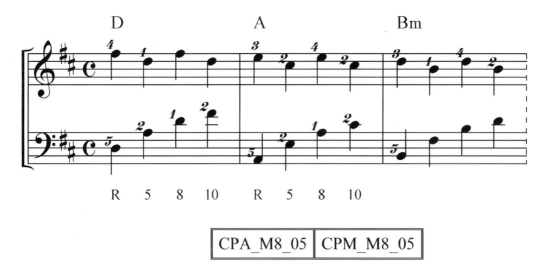

| CPA_M8_05 | CPM_M8_05 |

Continue the pattern right through the chord sequence:

:D	A	Bm	F#m	G	D	G	A :

Thirds with next-door notes

Next, keep the broken third but add a 'next-door note'

CPA_M8_06	CPM_M8_06

Again, the special fingering makes playing the version easy. Try to see fingering as a solution rather than as a problem – something that makes playing sweet music possible, rather than an irrelevant chore.

Audio Challenge

One option for developing this pattern is demonstrated in this audio example:

CPA_M8_07	CPM_M8_07

Try playing the version by just copying the audio performance. It should be familiar – it's actually a two-handed pattern from Module Two with the thirds broken up and rolled.

This version sounds rather mechanical – it needs more variety. Here's one possibility:

CPA_M8_08	CPM_M8_08

We can use arrows to make the movement of the top line easier to 'see' and remember.

→   Melody stays the same (note repeats)

↗   Melody goes up to the next note

↘   Melody goes down to the next note

This new version is a two-bar pattern. Using arrows alone to describe the movement, the top line of music (ignoring the lower note of the thirds) looks like this:

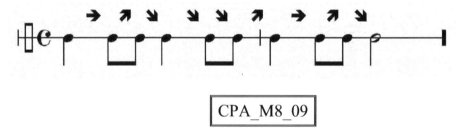

CPA_M8_09

You start on F sharp. The first note of each two-bar pattern is the third of the chord – note D for the B minor chord, note B for the G chord (twice). All the up and down arrows point to next-door notes.

To smooth out the melody line the last two bars (chords G and A) have to be adjusted, because the roots move up from G to A (and to D to repeat). Start on note B, chord G.

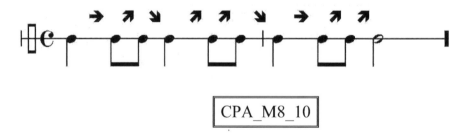

CPA_M8_10

Hearing the 'contour' (the vertical shape) of a melody line as a series of 'same' 'up' or 'down' movements is an important part of building your 'playing by ear' skills. Think of using arrows as a form of shorthand to sketch out (and make a record of) your own or someone else's melody lines.

The written-out music for the full chorus is in the 'Answers' section at the end of the book. See if you can keep in time with a slow drum backing track like CBT_D08.

> **Study tip** Always have a pencil by your keyboard and never be afraid to write on music – you can always rub it out! Write in your contour arrows, BMT (bottom, middle, top) coding. TLR (together, left, right) analysis (see below), the counts, fingering – anything! Just thinking about what you're going to write makes you think hard about what you're playing – a good thing!

'Together, left, right' (TLR) analysis

You can make a very nice Canon variation just by syncopating the thirds.

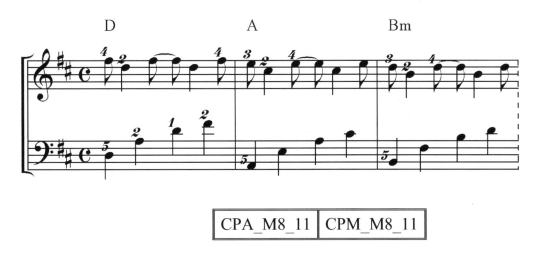

| CPA_M8_11 | CPM_M8_11 |

When you have to tackle a complicated rhythm like this, stop and look-and-listen closely until you're sure you know 'what comes with what' – whether your hands play together (T), or just the left hand (L) plays, or just the right (R).

This is 'Together, left, right' (TLR) analysis.

To learn to play such a pattern, abandon the rhythm temporarily and concentrate on finding the notes and getting the together, left, right 'events' in the right order, Then, gradually 'feed' the rhythm and tempo back in.

Here the TLR analysis (and the counting) for the solo syncopated thirds performance.

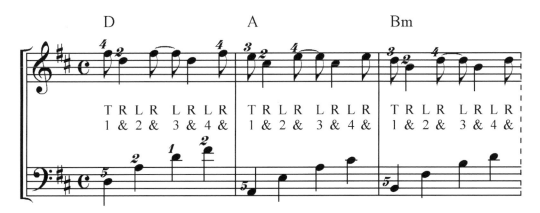

You play something on every quaver beat, but you only play hands together on count "one".

Finish off the version. Perhaps you can see now how the new fingering helps you play a legato treble part.

CPA_M8_11	CPM_M8_11

ACCOMPANIMENT WITH RIGHT HAND TRIADS

Now you have started playing your own full left hand accompaniment, your next step is playing along with broken-chord triads in the right hand. But the same accompaniment pattern doesn't work for all treble parts. It's easy to fix the problem by changing the order of your accompaniment pattern notes, and this will make you a lot more confident about creating your own root-fifth-octave-tenth accompaniments.

Here is the module audio performance.

CPA_M9_01

Right hand triads with left hand accompaniments

Revise the right hand triad (three-note chord) string from Module Three. Play the chords with a one-note bass line:

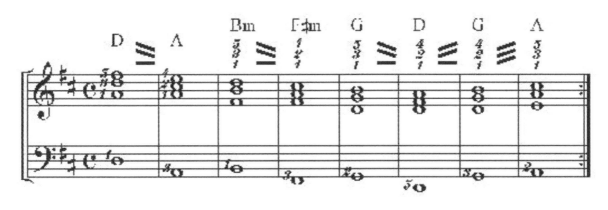

| CPA_M9_02 | CPM_M9_02 |

Now build the root, fifth, octave, tenth (R, 5, 8, 10) ladder on each bass note in turn.

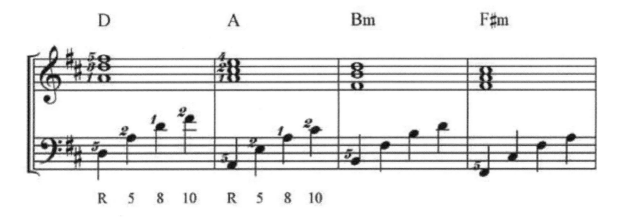

Finish the chord sequence using the chord chart:

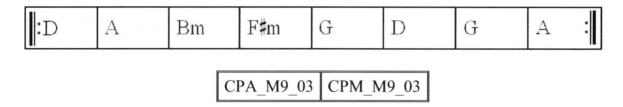

CPA_M9_03	CPM_M9_03

Broken-chord triads in the right hand

Recall the right hand broken chord pattern from Module Five. Here's the example we will be using:

CPA_M9_04	CPM_M9_04

Note that:

- This is a two-bar repeating bottom, middle, top (BMT) pattern:

$$\|: T \quad M \quad B \quad T \quad | T \quad M \quad B \quad :\|$$

- The semibreve (whole note) chords in the first two bars of the music example are there just to show you what chord to prepare – you don't play them.

Rehearse the pattern with a single-note bass line.

Now play the broken-chord triads over the R, 5, 8, 10 left hand accompaniment. The audio performance file is right after the next piece of written-out music, which shows the right hand triads as whole notes with the broken chord pattern in BMT coding. As a free-playing keyboard musician, you want to move to a position where you almost-automatically break up right hand triads into interesting, repeating patterns.

| CPA_M9_05 | CPM_M9_05 | CBT_02 |

'Bald spots'

This is a nice version and a good achievement, but the combination of left hand and right hand chord tones creates 'bald spots'. Listen again to the audio performance, and compare it with the improved version immediately below.

| CPA_M9_05 | CPM_M9_05 |

| CPA_M9_06 | CPM_M9_06 |

'Bald spots' occur where there are too many roots and fifths coming together, and the listener has to wait too long to hear the third/tenth (the third is the 'sweet' note in a triad). Playing the third (tenth) in both hands at the same time also makes a bald spot. The bald spots are corrected in the second version by changing the order of the notes in the left hand. Listen the two versions one after the other until you can hear the improvement.

The new LH accompaniment pattern

In the improved (second) version of the accompaniment, the left hand plays R, 5, 10, 8 instead of the standard R, 5, 8, 10 pattern – the last two chord tones are switched around.

73

(Read again, and check that you understand.) Here is the written-out music for the new left hand accompaniment pattern.

Practise this new R, 5, 10, 8 accompaniment pattern.

Notice that the fingering has changed. Don't try to hold onto the root or the fifth – use the sustain pedal to hold the notes and let your hand move freely to get to the tenth. Expect to practice a good deal.

Add the RH triads (whole chords) back in.

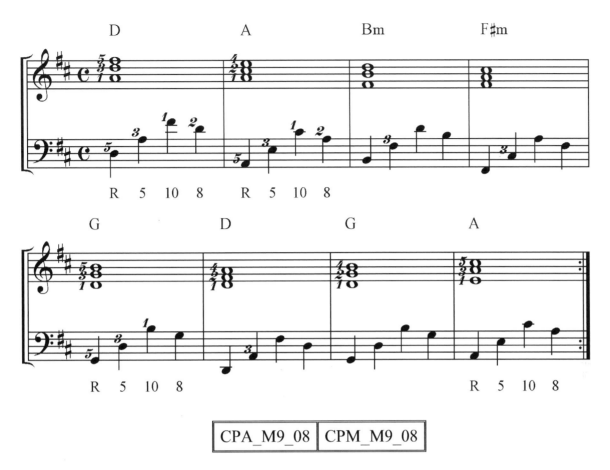

| CPA_M9_08 | CPM_M9_08 |

As soon as you add the right hand triads back in, you will see if your left hand R, 5, 10, 8 pattern needs more practice! When you can play the new LH accompaniment pattern and the straight triads together comfortably, play the RH broken chord pattern over the new accompaniment.

| CPA_M9_06 | CPM_M9_06 |

Compare the sound you have now with the old 'bald spot' version. You will hear that it's been worth the trouble.

| CPA_M9_05 | CPM_M9_05 |

Accompaniment patterns often have to be 'tweaked' like this in the light of what the right hand is playing. We explore this further in the next Canon Project module. Most left hand accompaniment patterns are made of the root, fifth, octave and tenth of the presiding chord, so time spent playing around with them is never wasted.

Using musical shorthand

Look at the last music example again. There's a great deal of information in it. Here it is, labelled.

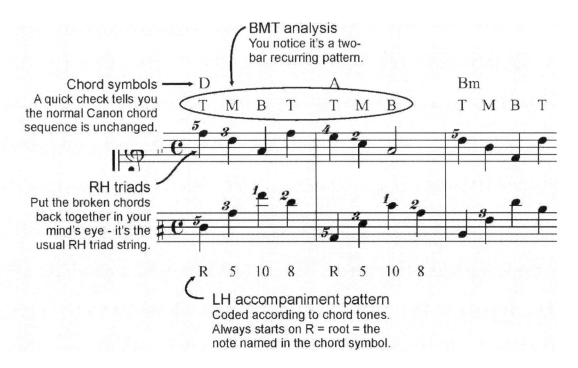

Written music tends to work against development of musical creativity because 'the dots' monopolise your brain. Unless you work hard at it, you don't have the attention left to spot the patterns. If you see through the dots to the patterns, you get to 'own' the music, and learn to play in a much more creative way.

Pachelbel's Canon is made up of patterns which express a simple but very pleasing chord sequence, and this makes it an excellent piece to focus on patterns and develop your creativity. Here is the information in the music above with 'the dots' removed altogether.

BMT	T M B T T M B	(two-bar pattern, recurring; usual RH triad string)					
Chord	D	A	Bm	F♯m	G	D	G	A
Accomp	R 5 10 8	(one-bar pattern, recurring)					

Study the table until it makes sense to you. The 'usual triad string' is this familiar music:

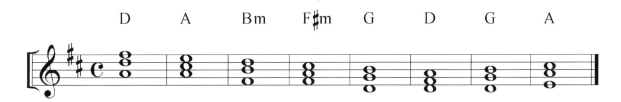

The first chord is a D major triad with F sharp as the top note, the second chord is an A major with E as the top note, and so on. We can express this in shorthand as well:

Top note	f sharp	e	d	c sharp	b	a	b	c sharp
Chord	D	A	Bm	F♯m	G	D	G	A

Feed that into the table:

BMT	T M B T T M B	(two-bar pattern, recurring; usual RH triad string)						
top note	f sharp	e	d	c sharp	b	a	b	c sharp
Chord	D	A	Bm	F♯m	G	D	G	A
Accomp	R 5 10 8	(one-bar pattern, recurring)						

This is a picture of how creative musicians 'think'. Try to play the final Module Nine version from this table alone.

Writing music out in full is time-consuming and laborious, but without some written record, it's easy to forget what you have done. Consider sketching your own compositions this way, using all the kinds of shorthand demonstrated.

Transposing challenge (optional)

One advantage of examining a chord sequence as thoroughly as the Musicarta Canon Project does, is that the in-depth knowledge about chords and chord sequences you acquire 'spins off' into all your playing.

'Transposing' – easily playing music you know in a different key – is a great way to practise this advanced benefit.

If you work through the Canon Project Transposing mini-series on the home musicarta.com site, you will learn the Roman numeral system of naming chords, and then you will be able to see even deeper into the chord structure and read the module performance like this:

BMT	T M B T T M B	(two-bar pattern, recurring; usual RH triad string)						
top note	3rd	5th	3rd	5th	3rd	5th	3rd	3rd
Chord	I	V	vi	iii	IV	I	IV	V
Accomp	R 5 10 8	(one-bar pattern, recurring)						

The chords of the Canon chord sequence are now expressed as Roman numerals – they are 'the chords in any key'. There is a full briefing on the Roman numeral system of naming chords in the first module of the Canon Project Transposing mini-series on the

Musicarta site. If you are committed to learning how harmony works, this system is highly recommended.

Here is a transposing table for D major to C major.

Key: D	D	Em	F♯m	G	A	Bm	C♯dim
RNS	I	ii	iii	IV	V	vi	vii°
Key: C	C	Dm	Em	F	G	Am	Bdim

In the Roman numeral system, the Canon chord sequence is this:

Canon (RNS)	I	V	vi	iii	IV	I	IV	V

Read those Roman numerals off in the key of D in the table above, and you will see the familiar D, A, Bm, F♯m, G, D, G, A chord sequence emerging.

Your transposing challenge is to transpose the Canon Module Nine performance into C major. Follow a logical step-by-step build-up:

- Using the two tables above, find out what the Canon chords are in the key of C major. Write them out in ordinary chord symbols if you need to and rehearse.

- Find the familiar-shaped bass line (roots – the notes of the chord symbol letters). Play it with the 'usual string' of right hand triads (in C) from above.

- Find and rehearse the original R, 5, 8, 10 accompaniment pattern in C. Find the right hand chords (the 'usual RH triad string') and break them up in the two-bar T M B T | T M B pattern.

- Put the hands together.

- Change the left hand accompaniment chord tones to R, 5, 10, 8 for the 'improved version'.

This what your finished version should sound like:

CPA_M9_10	CPM_M9_10	CBT_02

Expect to take a number of sessions to accomplish this. Each of the bullet points above is a 'tick-box task' on its own. As a minimum, play the basic Canon chord sequence triads in C major with a single-note bass line.

MIXED ACCOMPANIMENT PATTERNS

In the last module, you discovered that the same left hand accompaniment pattern doesn't necessarily suit all right hand music. In this module, you train your ear to recognize more 'bald spots' that need fixing, and get more practice on root-fifth-octave-tenth accompaniment patterns – the raw material of most solo accompaniments.

Here is the module audio performance, demonstrating an improved mixed-type accompaniment pattern.

CPA_M10_01

Earlier treble parts with accompaniment

Rehearse this right hand triad pattern.

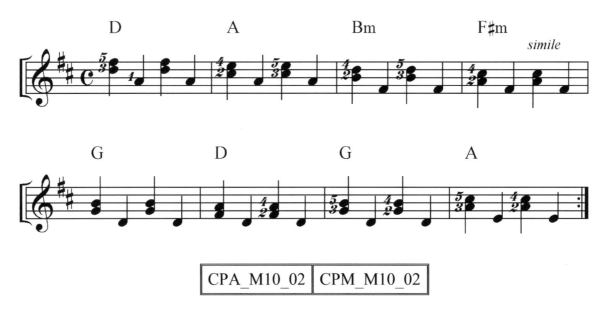

CPA_M10_02 | CPM_M10_02

Notice how the fingering changes within the bar to prepare the next chord. The '*simile*' marking at the end of the first line – Italian for 'the same' – tells you to continue using the same fingering solution.

At the low D chord, you change direction, so the 'solution' goes into reverse.

Play the right hand pattern over the original R, 5, 8, 10 accompaniment. Use backing track CBT_02.

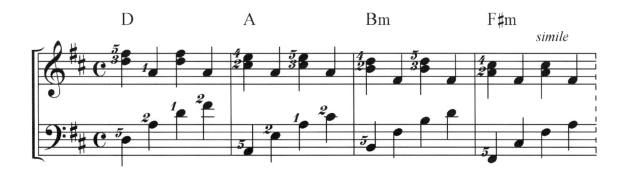

Complete the chord sequence.

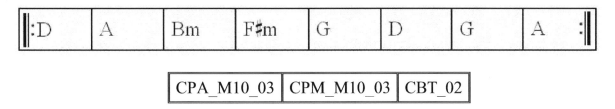

:D	A	Bm	F♯m	G	D	G	A :

CPA_M10_03	CPM_M10_03	CBT_02

Do you hear any 'bald spots' that need fixing?

There are none. We are not kept waiting – listening to 'bald' roots, fifths and octaves – to hear a third (the 'sweet' chord tone), and the third is not doubled (played in both hands at the same time) either. There is no need to adapt the accompaniment and this variation can go straight into your 'ready to play' list.

More LH–RH combinations

Revise this Module Five broken chord pattern.

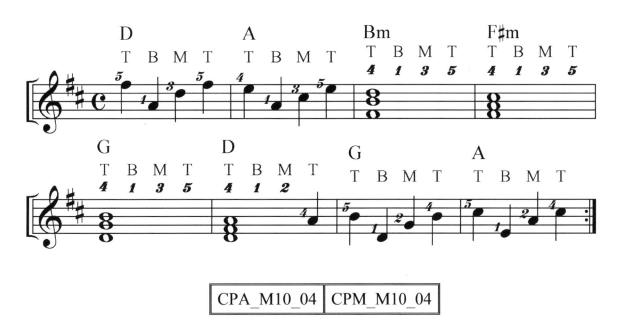

CPA_M10_04	CPM_M10_04

The audio performance file plays the broken chord pattern over a single-note bass line. (It's always a good idea to build up to creative music-making by rehearsing and then assembling blocks of simpler material you can easily achieve.)

When you have the pattern secure, play it over the standard left hand accompaniment pattern.

CPA_M10_05	CPM_M10_05

Now you hear some glaring bald spots. The right hand plays exactly the same notes for most of the odd-numbered bars. To adjust the accompaniment you will want to play the alternative R, 5, 10, 8 pattern in the odd-numbered bars. We will practice mixing left hand accompaniment patterns on their own first, before playing hands together.

Mixed-type accompaniment patterns

The best way to learn mixed accompaniment patterns is to play them with two hands first. These mixed patterns are quite pleasing on their own. Play them with your classical Canon recordings in the background, or as the bass (secondo) part of a duet.

First, revise the two accompaniment types using hands L, R, R, R.

CPA_M10_06	CPM_M10_06

Here's the second, R, 5, 10, 8 type:

| CPA_M10_07 | CPM_M10_07 |

Now play a chorus of the Canon chord sequence starting with the altered R, 5, 10, 8 version in the odd-numbered bars and original R, 5, 8, 10 in the even bars. (Use the altered R, 5, 10, 8 version in bar 8, though. You will see why later.)

| CPA_M10_08 | CPM_M10_08 |

Next, play the 'mixed type' accompaniment with the left hand alone, with simple triads in the treble.

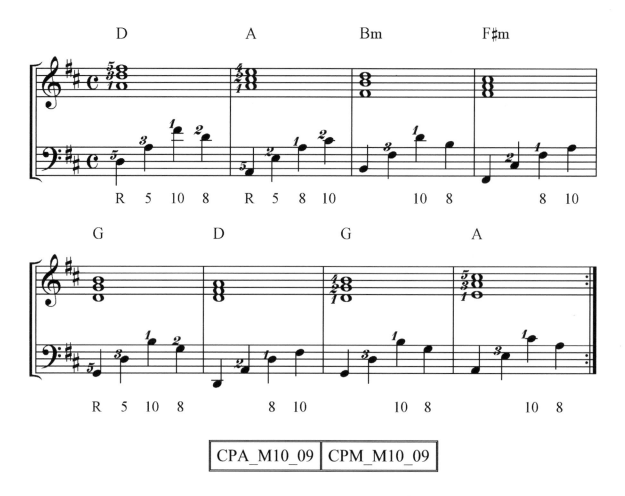

CPA_M10_09 | CPM_M10_09

Broken chords over mixed accompaniment patterns

Finally, break up the right hand triads in the broken-chord pattern we are using…

‖: T B M T | T B M T :‖

… and play the broken chords over the mixed-type accompaniment.

| CPA_M10_01 | CPM_M10_01 |

Compare this with the original R, 5, 8, 10 all-the-way-through version to hear how the 'bald spots' have been cured.

| CPA_M10_05 | CPM_M10_05 |

Audio challenge

Here is our latest version filled out with some 'in-between notes' in the even-numbered bars. See if you can work out by ear what they are and play the new version.

| CPA_M10_10 |

The music and the MIDI file reference number are in the 'Answers' section. You can always try squeezing in (or substituting) some 'next door notes' in your own variations. Use backing track CBT_02 to support your performance.

Selecting mixed-type accompaniments yourself

Selecting what accompaniment goes best with a right hand pattern involves listening closely and exercising your artistic judgement – it is an introduction to musical 'arrangement'.

Here are some treble patterns from earlier modules. Practice them first, then decide whether they require R, 5, 8, 10 or R, 5, 10, 8 or mixed-type accompaniment.

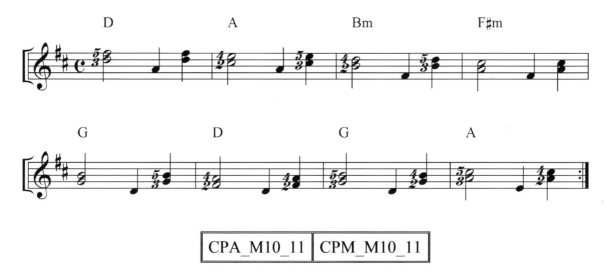

CPA_M10_11 | CPM_M10_11

Suppose you had a slight variation of this pattern in the next chorus:

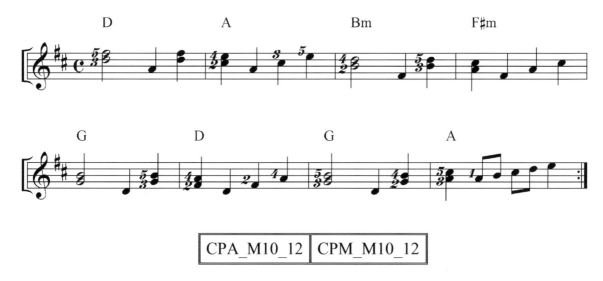

CPA_M10_12 | CPM_M10_12

What accompaniment would best suit that right hand part? Join the two choruses together and play with your chosen accompaniment types. You can find the music and the audio and MIDI performance file references in the 'Answers' section at the back of the book.

What left hand pattern or combination of patterns suits the following right hand material best?

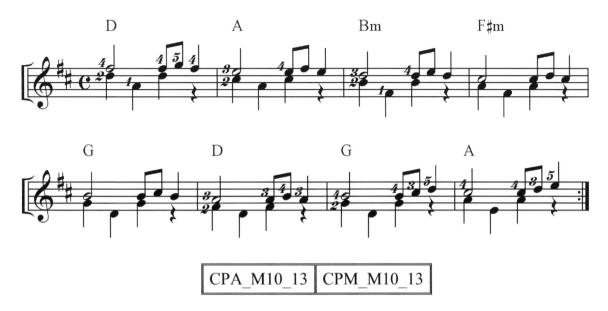

| CPA_M10_13 | CPM_M10_13 |

What do you think the best accompaniment pattern for the following broken chord pattern (using the usual right hand triads) would be?

$$\|{:}\ T\ M\ B\ T\ |\ T\ M\ B\ T\ :\|$$

Find the suggested solutions in the 'Answers' section.

More 'mixed-type' accompaniments

Here is a table version of another mixed-type two-handed accompaniment.

Chord	D	A	Bm	F♯m	G	D
Hands	L R R R	L R R R	(always L R R R)			
Chord-tone	R 10 5 8	R 5 8 10	R 10 5 8	R 5 8 10	(two-bar repeating)	

Note the two-bar chord-tone pattern: R, 10, 5, 8 │R, 5, 8, 10. Complete the chord sequence using the same two-bar pattern.

‖:D	A	Bm	F♯m	G	D	G	A :‖

This pattern sounds very pleasant just on its own, and would also be useful as the lower part of a duet (the 'secondo'). Try playing it from the table, then check your performance in the 'Answers' section.

SUSPENSIONS

You can easily get more out of any chord sequence by pulling some of the chord tones up one scale step temporarily, then letting them fall back. In music theory, this is called 'suspension and resolution'.

Here is the performance you will learn in this module:

> CPA_M11_01

Suspensions in the Canon chord sequence

If you listen carefully to any classical Canon recording, about two thirds of the way through you will hear the music do something like this:

> CPA_M11_02 | CPM_M11_02

What is happening is that the middle note of each right hand triad is being pulled up a step (the 'suspension' – 'sus') and then let drop back down to its original position (the 'resolution' – 'res').

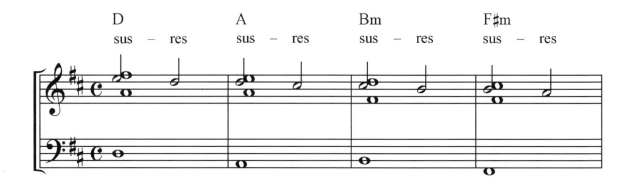

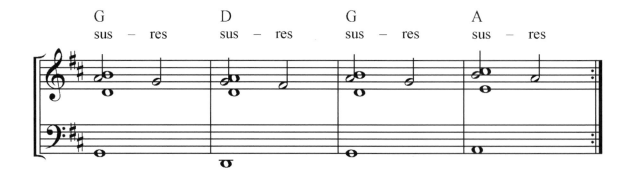

To make this quite clear, copy the next audio clip. Use two hands, as in the music (left hand stems down, right hand stems up) and the MIDI file, so you can concentrate on what's happening to the chord instead of wrestling with the fingering.

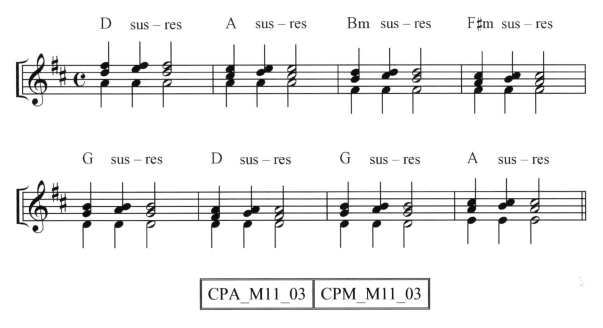

Pachelbel's Canon goes straight into the 'suspension' chord – the second chord in each of the groups above. Technically speaking, this is called an 'unprepared' suspension.

You can 'roll' the 'sus – res' chords using two hands.

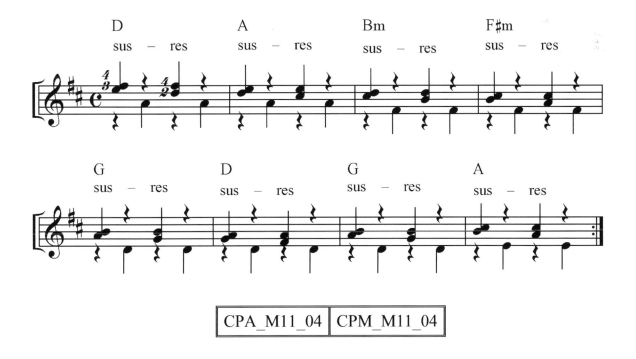

Note that the music above is written as simply as possible and the audio and MIDI files play it exactly as written. In practice, you make your fingers 'sticky' and hold the notes as long as possible, like this:

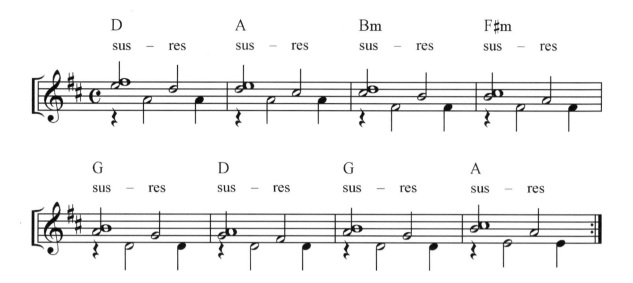

The top note of the triad is even held for the whole bar, not played twice. The result is a more lush sound, as the following audio and MIDI files show.

| CPA_M11_05 | CPM_M11_05 |

This would sound good as the 'primo' (upper) part of a duet performance. What accompaniment pattern would you ask your 'secondo' to play?

A solo performance

Learn to play the rolled chords with just the right hand:

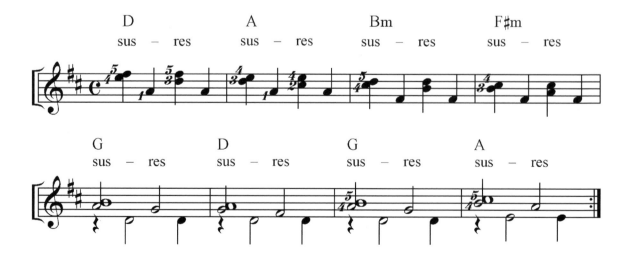

| CPA_M11_06 | CPM_M11_06 |

The top line of music shows the music written as simply as possible. It would be quite all right for you to play this version.

The bottom line shows a really 'legato' performance, with tied notes (as in the audio and MIDI performances). Study the fingering options – the fingering makes more advanced effects like these possible.

Then play this right hand over the standard R, 5, 8, 10 left hand accompaniment.

| CPA_M11_07 | CPM_M11_07 | CBT_03 |

Suspensions with mixed accompaniment

If you listen carefully to the previous audio clip, you can hear a 'bald spot' in the odd-numbered bars, where both hands play the fifth and the root at the same time.

This is easily fixed by playing a R, 5, 10, 8 accompaniment pattern in the odd-numbered bars and the standard R, 5, 8, 10 pattern in the even-numbered bars. (You learnt this mixed-type accompaniment in Module Ten.)

| CPA_M11_01 | CPM_M11_01 |

Compare this with the original, 'bald spot' version, listening hard for the improvement.

| CPA_M11_07 | CPM_M11_07 |

Most of the recorded music you hear will have had many, many of these little improvements incorporated. Start training your ear to hear where an arrangement needs this kind of attention.

A duet version

You can use the mixed-types two-handed accompaniment as a secondo duet part. The MIDI file indicated in the table below shows both the primo and secondo correctly assigned to left and right hands. It will sound just like the module audio performance.

| CPA_M11_01 | CPM_M11_11 |

The suspensions played 'straight'

Most pupils find it more difficult to play the suspensions 'straight' (three notes all together) than it is to roll them. See if you can finger the three-note suspension-resolutions as shown here:

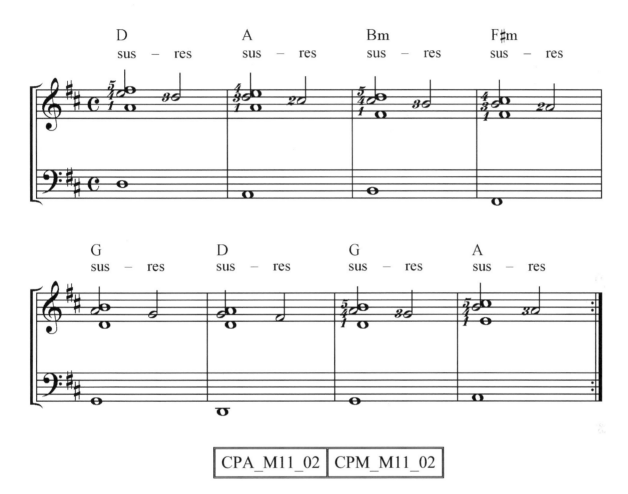

| CPA_M11_02 | CPM_M11_02 |

You notice that, when we're learning something new like this, we simplify things by, for example, playing just a single-note bass line.

You might want to adopt a slightly different fingering – the fingering in the example above is very 'classical.'

When you have made some progress, try the three-note suspension-resolution chords with the mixed-type accompaniment which avoids 'bald spots'.

CPA_M11_10 | CPM_M11_10

You will get more practice playing the three-note suspension-resolution chords in the module audio and transposing challenges which follow.

Audio challenge

Here is a build-up to a simple but catchy riff using just the D and A major suspension-resolutions in the centre of the keyboard with a simple bass line.

See if you can learn it by ear. The suspension – resolution pairs are just the same as in the first two bars of Canon, but an octave lower.

Remember that both Windows Media Player and MidiPiano can be set to repeat (and slow down) the performance file, giving you lots of time to learn the riff by simply copying.

CPA_M11_12

Use the written-out music and the MIDI file in the 'Answers' section to check your performance. Use a backing track to support your performance.

Transposing challenge

Listen to this performance of the Canon chord sequence – with suspensions – in F. Your challenge is to copy it.

CPA_M11_13

Here is a D to F Roman numeral system (RNS) transposing table:

Key: D	D	Em	F♯m	G	A	Bm	C♯dim
RNS	I	ii	iii	IV	V	vi	vii°
Key: F	F	Gm	Am	B♭	C	Dm	Edim

In the Roman numeral system, the Canon chord sequence is:

Canon (RNS)	I	V	vi	iii	IV	I	IV	V

Use the step-by-step transposing process you used in Module Nine.

- Read the Roman numerals off in the bottom row of the transposing table to get the Canon chord sequence in F. Find the correct right hand inversions – the ones that look like the 'usual RH triad string'.

- Find the familiar-shaped single-note bass line (roots – the notes of the chord symbol letters). Play it with the right hand triads.

- Pull the middle note of each triad up one F major scale degree to create the suspension, then let it drop to its original position (the resolution).

- Copy the feel of the F major audio performance, especially the slightly funky bass line 'kicks'.

Check your performance against the written-out music and the MIDI file in the 'Answers' section.

Note how useful it is to know your scales. (This is one big advantage of the classical exam curriculum.) You can learn scales just to be good at scales, but the real reason for the modern keyboard player to learn scales is to learn the keys. Some arrangements just 'sound right' in a certain key, vocalists can often only sing a song in one key and so on, so playing well in different keys is a 'fact of life' for pro and semi-pro musicians. Pop musicians should ideally put themselves on a scales program, so as not to be caught out when the time comes! Visit the Scales tab at musicarta.com for some ideas to liven up your scales practice.

Suspensions in popular music

This is a very brief introduction to suspensions. For example, if you look at the Canon suspensions closely, you will see that the chord tone that is being 'suspended' is not always the same one. In the D, B minor, G and final A chords, it is the root that is pulled up and then released. This is called a 2 – 1 suspension. In the other bars, it is the third which is suspended. These are 4 – 3 suspensions – the more common type.

In popular music, suspensions are usually indicated by 'sus' in a chord symbol – Dsus, for example. This would usually indicate a 4 – 3 suspension/resolution. (Sometimes you will see 'sus4' in the chord symbol, which is more informative.) A 2 – 1 suspension will sometimes be indicated loosely (if at all) by 'add 9' or 'add 2'.

In popular sheet music, the resolution is not normally indicated with the 'res' provided in this Musicarta module, although sometimes a plain 'D' chord symbol (in our example) would show that the suspension had resolved.

Keep working at bringing your theory knowledge to bear! Experiment with suspensions in a general way. Move your chord tones about, one scale-tone either side. Naturally, you need to be staying on the one chord for a few beats for there to be enough time for a suspension/resolution pair. You will find a wealth of new sounds in any chord progression. Use the voice movement diagrams on page 32 to think about and notate your experiments.

There is a 'Suspensions' tab on the Musicarta site nav bar which will lead you through to more suspensions material – and a Suspensions playlist at Mister Musicarta YouTube, too.

Suffering from project fatigue?

Are you suffering from 'Canon Project fatigue'?

Take heart! By now, you're not really just learning the Canon any more – you're actually flexing your very own creative muscles.

It's easy to flit from one thing to another in the interests of variety, learning this riff and that, but real understanding comes from taking just one thing and knowing it inside out – especially a 'core' chord sequence like the Canon.

Because it is so 'typical', studying the Canon chord sequence thoroughly is very fruitful. Once you can compose or improvise Canon variations – by finishing versions suggested in this volume, for example, and just generally 'messing about' with the Canon chords – the many similar chord sequences that crop up in popular music will be 'child's play' to you.

As you advance from module to module, you will find more and more 'branching out' exercises which will prove how valuable your commitment to the Canon Project is. So, stay with the programme – real expertise is being built from your daily inputs!

SLASH CHORDS

As with suspensions, you can get more out of any chord sequence by using a note other than the root in the bass line. This note will usually be the third or the fifth of the chord. This results in a chord known as a 'slash chord', written, for example, A/C♯ (say "A over C sharp" or "A with C sharp in the bass") which indicates that the bass (left hand) note is a C sharp, while the whole chord (both hands together) is an A major chord.

Here is a sample of textures based on the material you will learn in this module. Listen particularly to the bass line.

CPA_M12_01

Finding the slash chord bass notes

Play the string of thirds from Module One of the Canon Project. Use two hands. (The next audio file below covers the whole three-step process.)

Take the left hand down an octave:

You are now playing 'tenths' – a third plus an octave. Take the left hand down another octave:

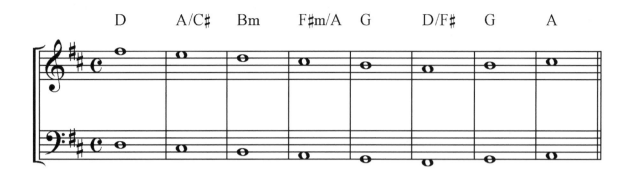

CPA_M12_02	CPM_M12_02

You have your new bass line, and the chord symbols reflect this – "A over C sharp", "F sharp minor over A", "D over F sharp". The new bass line moves in scale steps; it is smoothed out, which is usually considered a 'good thing' in music.

Playing the triads with the new bass line

Find the usual right hand triads in the centre of the keyboard and put them over the new bass line.

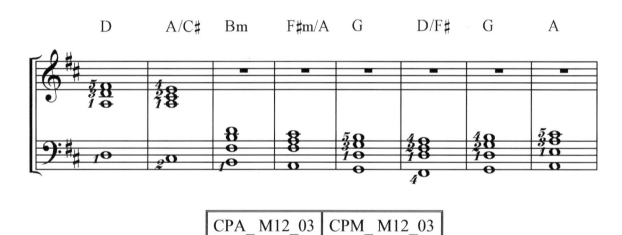

CPA_M12_03	CPM_M12_03

Play the right hand chords according to this BMT 'recipe' (it's from Module Ten):

‖: T B M T | T B M T :‖

… over the new bass line.

CPA_M12_04	CPM_M12_04	CBT_D04

Here is a 'sketch' of the music, but first, try to play without it. The first two chords are shown 'prepared' (as whole notes) and broken up; after that, you see just the chord and the broken chord BMT coding.

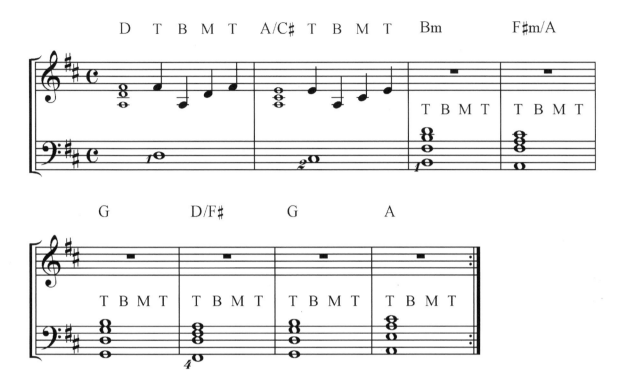

This version makes up the second chorus (8 bars) of the module audio performance.

Audio challenge

See if you can play this broken-chord variation of the RH chords over the new step-wise bass line:

CPA_M12_05	CPM_M12_05

The right hand BMT pattern is this:

‖: T B T M | T B M T :‖

The last two chords (G and A) are 'tweaked' quite a bit. The right hand G chord is a root position chord (root, third, fifth) and the hands in the last bar (A chord) walk in parallel back to the starting position.

You can find the written-out music and the MIDI file reference number in the 'Answers' section, if you need them.

Re-voicing the right hand Canon chords

In previous modules we changed the accompaniment to fit better with the right hand music. Now that we are featuring the bass line, we are going to adapt the right hand pattern to avoid over-balancing the music with 'doubling' (playing too many of the same note together at one time).

Listen to this portion of the module performance and study the illustrations which follow.

| CPA_M12_06 | CPM_M12_06 |

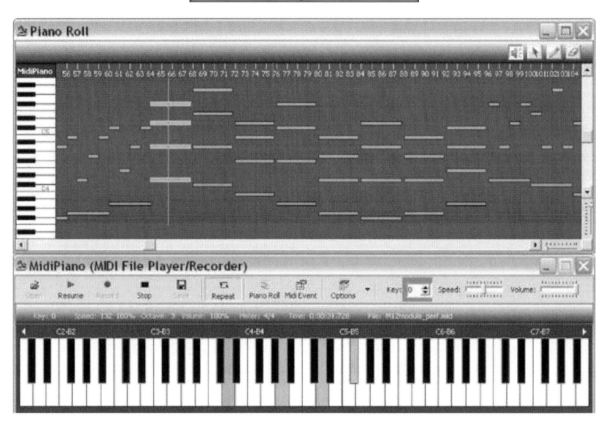

The illustration shows the relevant portion of the module MIDI performance file played on MidiPiano. The performance is paused on the first D chord, which you can see in piano roll pane and lit up on the keyboard.

Here is a snapshot of all eight chords in the re-voiced chord sequence.

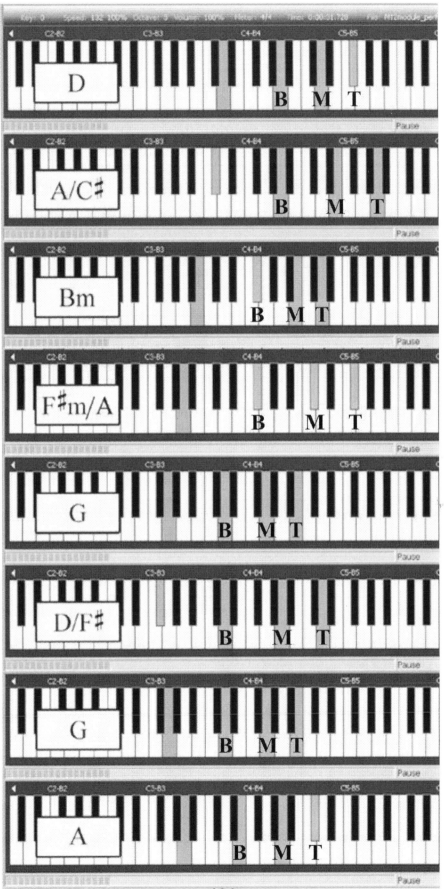

You can see from this illustration how MidiPiano can help you learn to see chords in the keyboard, without having to go through written music.

Here is the music for the new chord voicings, used in the third chorus of the module performance.

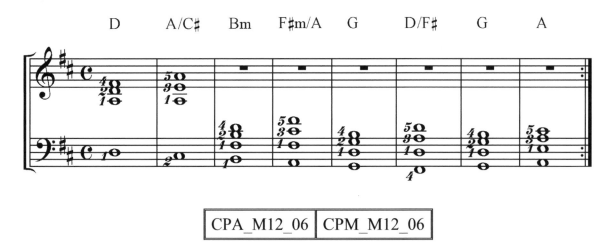

| CPA_M12_06 | CPM_M12_06 |

In the re-voiced chords (bars 2, 4 and 6), the third appears only in the bass – the 'doubled third' in the right hand has been 'cured'. (Too many thirds in a chord are considered a 'bad thing' – they tend to over-balance the chord.) All chords now have two roots, one fifth and one third (tenth), which is considered the best selection for a four-note chord.

The new right hand chords in broken-chord patterns

Next, break up the new RH chords according to this pattern:

‖: T B M T | M B T B :‖

| CPA_M12_07 | CPM_M12_07 | CBT_D04 |

Note that the last two chords/bars (G and A) are still in the old pattern:

‖: T B M T | T B M T :‖

For maximum benefit, go back to the keyboard illustration on the previous page and play the broken-chord pattern arrangement you hear in the audio clip. To help you, the chord tones on the keyboards in the illustration are labelled B, M, T.

Or work from this sketch music:

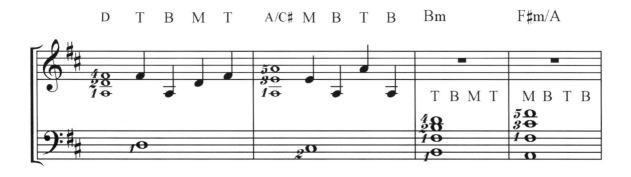

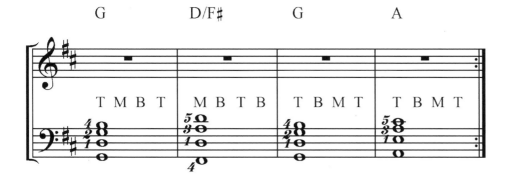

Developing the bass line

Now we break the bass line up. Play octaves and split the whole notes (semibreves) into bottom, top, top, bottom half-notes (minims), two per bar. Play straight right hand chord (new voicings) while you learn the new bass line (first chorus of the audio), then break up the right hand chords as before (second chorus of the audio).

CPA_M12_08	CPM_M12_08

Here is the sketch music:

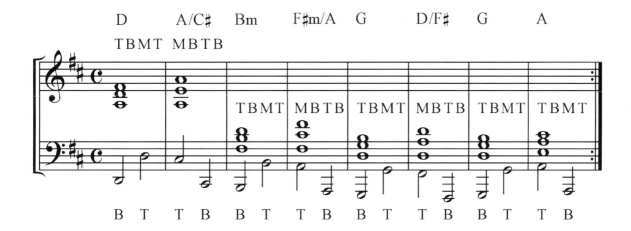

103

Don't let yourself be distracted into puzzling over the bass clef leger lines. 'Slash bass' symbols are there to tell you if a note other than the root is in the bass. If there is a slash bass chord symbol, both notes in the bass/left hand are the notes after the slash – C sharp, A and F sharp in bars 2, 4 and 6.

If there isn't a slash bass indicated, the bass note is the root – the note named in the chord symbol.

Go back and deliberately pay attention to the BMT coding in the example above. Can you hear the chords and break them up in your 'mind's ear'? The more often you deliberately 'go through the motions' like this, the closer you get to the music just spontaneously happening.

Finally, study how the 'tune' in the last two choruses of the module performance springs out of the broken chord pattern in the last musical example. Some notes get 'promoted' to melody notes by

- being played louder and held longer, and
- being joined up with next-door-note preparations and runs.

This audio clip should make the process clearer:

CPA_M12_09

Transposing challenge

If you have worked through the <u>Canon Project Transposing mini-series</u> on the home Musicarta site, you should be able to tackle this transposing exercise.

Listen to this audio file:

CPA_M12_10

The audio file is in five sections. See if you can follow this work flow.

Section One

   Transpose the 'usual right hand triads' into G.

CPA_M12_10a

Section Two

   Find the new smoothed-out next-door-note bass line (from G).

CPA_M12_10b

Section Three

Put the hands together, but use only the top and bottom notes of the right hand chords, so you have chords with three notes in total.

CPA_M12_10c

Section Four

Break up the right hand two-note chord according to the pattern you hear in this audio performance:

CPA_M12_10d

Section Five

Change the chord sequence a little by 'reversing' from E minor back to the beginning twice before going on. The chord sequence of Section Five is:

G	D/F♯	Em	D/F♯	G	D/F♯	Em	D/F♯
G	D/F♯	Em	Bm/D	C	D	C	D

CPA_M12_10e

This last adaptation is called 'harmonic variation' – the chord sequence itself can also be varied. You achieve this kind of creative freedom by knowing a chord sequence very well – and by being willing to take chances at the keyboard. You will be revisiting harmonic variation in Modules Fifteen and Sixteen.

MELODIC VARIATIONS

The Canon chord sequence is ideal for learning to create melodies around chord tones. One way to do this is to sketch out the 'contour' of a sample two-bar melodic fragment and identify what chord tone it starts on. The Canon chord sequence's regular structure allows you to fill out an entire eight-bar chorus by repeating the same fragment – with minor variations. A development of the melody fragment usually follows, and in this way a whole performance can be built up.

Here is the module performance.

CPA_M13_01	CPM_M13_01

Internal structure of the Canon chord sequence

The regular internal structure of the Canon chord sequence was pointed out when you were learning the bass line in Module Two. The essential points are:

1. There are four pairs of chords.

2. In the first three pairs of chords, the root falls a fourth.

3. The first three pairs overlap by one scale tone.

4. The last pair is a different, get-back-to-the-starting-place pair.

Play through any simple arrangement of the Canon chord sequence and check that you can identify these features. You will see them clearly in the bass line diagrams in the next section.

Describing melody by contour

One important aspect of a melody is its up/down shape, as seen from the side – its 'contour'.

Here is the familiar Canon bass line.

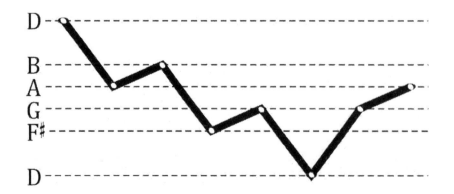

If we fill in the space underneath we get a silhouette, which gives a clearer picture of its contour.

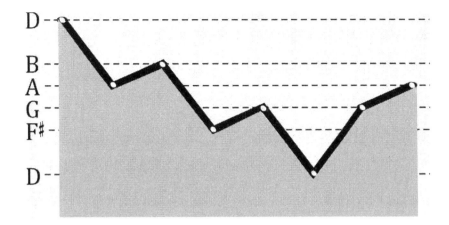

The simplest way to describe contour is to use arrows to indicate same, up or down movement between notes.

➔ Melody stays the same (note repeats)

↗ Melody goes up to the next note

↘ Melody goes down to the next note

Here is the bass line with the right arrows for the slopes of the silhouette (contour) put in:

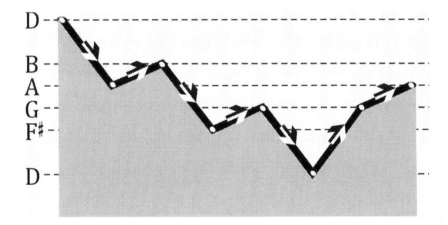

Here is the bass line as just a series of dots (representing the notes) with the contour arrows between them representing the up/down movement. (There isn't a 'stays-the-same' in the Canon bass line.) Play the bass line from this illustration, starting on D.

Note that the shorthand doesn't tell you how much higher or lower the next note is.

107

Describing melodic fragments by rhythm

Another obvious defining aspect of a melody is the rhythm of the notes.

Here is one chorus of the module performance:

CPA_M13_02

Listen carefully, a number of times. You want to first isolate the top line of notes (the melody) in your ear, then notate (or just remember) the rhythm of the melody notes.

This audio clip demonstrates the process over the course of just one Canon chorus.

CPA_M13_03

If we notate just the rhythm, we discover the four pairs of bars all have this rhythm:

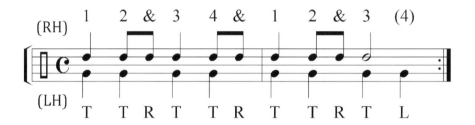

This is a Musicarta 'beat map', showing just the rhythm of the right and left hand notes of the fragment in the audio. Tap out the stems-up notes with your right hand and the stems-down notes with your left hand (and/or a foot, if you can). You should hear something like this:

CPA_M13_04

Establishing the contour of the melodic fragment

Copy out, right across a sheet of exam pad paper, the rhythmic pattern of the notes from the beat map above. It will look something like this:

This is the line of notes we want to sketch the 'contour' of by putting in the up, down or same arrows.

Listen again closely to the following performance clip – it's slowed down to help you as you try to put arrows between the notes to indicate whether the note stays the same (i.e. repeats), or the melody goes up or down to the next note.

CPA_M13_05

NB: For now, you are only listening to the first three pairs of chords: D–A, Bm–F#m and G–D.

You might be able to do this almost immediately or you might have to listen many times before you can identify the up/down/same shape. (If you can play it by ear immediately, it's because you have identified the 'contour'.)

You might find it easier to work from this clip – it's just the first melodic fragment (the first pair of chords) repeated.

CPA_M13_06

You can be fairly sure the fragment starts on a D major chord tone. If you play a D major triad up where the music plays, you can probably find which one. The up/down movements are not big, so play around with next-door notes (D major scale tones) and see if you can pin the up/down/same profile down.

Working at your aural (listening) skills away from the keyboard is highly recommended. Here are some helpful techniques.

1. Sing-and-listen to establish how many different pitches (heights of notes) there are in the fragment. There are ten notes in the fragment, but only _____ different pitches. (Working this out makes the task more manageable.)

2. As you listen, scribble a series of ten dots representing the notes across a piece of exam pad paper, with the higher notes higher up the page and the lower notes lower down the page. Exaggerate the up/down distance. Just guess (it's only paper!), and see if an up/down contour emerges.

3. Sing along and scribble the line of dots just as above. You don't have to be able to sing well or even remotely in tune – you can feel higher/lower/the same in your throat.

4. Close your eyes and stab the air in front of you according to whether you think the note is higher or lower. Again, your muscles help you think about the pitch.

Here's your sample again:

CPA_M13_06

This is the correct sequences of arrows.

Check your answer carefully. If you have something different, listen again to the test segment and 'see with your ears' where you've gone wrong. Correct your contour template.

Identify the starting note

We have now successfully 'contoured' the first melodic fragment. It covers two chords – D and A (first pair of chords, first two bars).

We have said that identifying the contour of the fragment will be useful because we can repeat it and easily get a whole chorus of music out of it. But to do this we need to know what note to start playing the fragment on (if you haven't already found out). You will want to be able to do this for yourself, by ear.

You can be fairly sure the fragment starts on a D major chord tone. If you play a D major triad up where the music plays, you can probably find which one. Try the chord tones in turn as you listen to or sing the first note of the melody fragment. Decide which chord tone the melody fragment starts on.

The melody fragment starts on note F sharp. The chord is D major – F sharp is the 'third' of D major.

Repeat the fragment contour

The melody fragment starts on the third (chord tone) of the first chord in the pair, so you will start playing the next melody fragment on the third of B minor, the first chord in the next pair. The third of B minor is note D.

Play the melody fragment in the right hand starting on note D, following the up/down/same arrows. All the notes are next-door notes (D major scale tones). Then put the B minor and F sharp minor R, 5, 8, 10 accompaniment patterns underneath it:

CPA_M13_07

The next pair of chords is G–D, so we play the melody fragment from 'the third of G'. (To find 'the third', count three letter names, including G.)

CPA_M13_08

You have now filled three-quarters of a whole chorus using your contour knowledge and the starting-note key.

Contour for the last pair of chords

Our examination of the Canon chord sequence structure revealed three pairs of chords the same (root falling a fourth) and one pair – the last pair – different. In the last pair of chords, the root rises from G to A; the melody will be different and we will have to discover the new 'contour'.

Go back to your blank rhythmic pattern and listen to the relevant portion of the audio performance file, here repeated to give you a better chance to hear the contour:

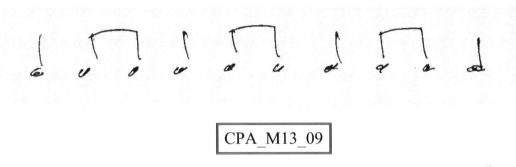

CPA_M13_09

Work at it until you're sure your arrows truly represent the up/down movement of the melody fragment.

This is the correct sequence of arrows:

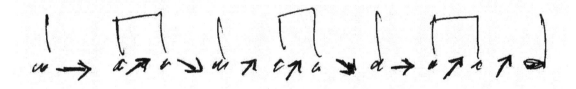

Check your answer carefully. If you have something different, listen again to the test segment until you 'see with your ears' where you've gone wrong. Correct your 'contour template'.

The whole 8-bar chorus as contour

Take plenty of time to look-and-listen to the following 'plan' of the module performance – the chorus you have just built up.

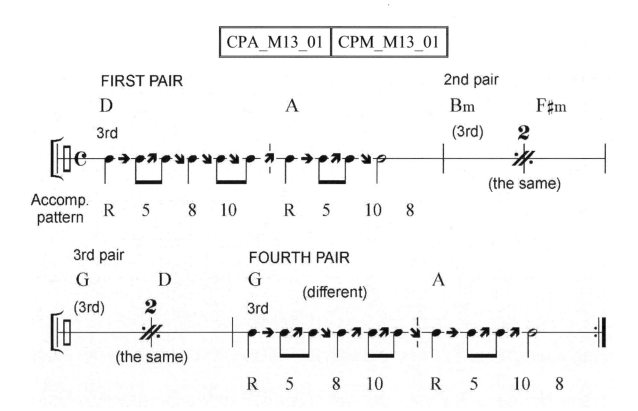

It shows the four pairs of chords with the melody fragment contour written out in full in the first pair. The next two pairs are 'the same' – the contour is the same and starts on the 3rd of the chord – but using different chords, of course. (Note the handy two-bar repeat mark.) The fourth pair is 'different' because the contour is different – but the melody still starts on the 3rd of the chord.

A mixed-type accompaniment pattern which avoids doubling is shown.

The illustration shows the thought processes and abilities of the improvising, creative keyboard player, and studying it will train up your independent creative powers. With practice you can read the illustration as music and hear the notes as you look at it.

Moving from 'reading the dots' to taking charge of the music-creating is a quantum leap for most musicians, and you might have to 'just sit with' this new kind of notation for quite a while before you see the point.

Audio challenge

These two choruses have exactly the same rhythm as the module example. Play them, using the method worked through above to assist you.

CPA_M13_10

CPA_M13_11

Select bass accompaniment patterns (R, 5, 8, 10 or R, 5, 10, 8) to avoid doubling the chord tones of the melodic line. The MIDI files and plans of the two choruses are in the 'Answers' section.

Improvising your own top line

Finally, listen to this improvisation on the module performance. It uses the step-wise 'slash' bass line with the bouncing bottom-top-top-bottom profile, and decorates the melody with 'ornaments' (trills and so on) and by delaying notes. It's quite classical, but also a bit jazzy.

CPA_M13_12

Try something similar yourself.

CANON PROJECT – MODULE FOURTEEN

NEW CHORDS AND MELODIES

Being able to make inversions of the chords in a chord sequence is a cornerstone of creative keyboard technique. Triads can be 'flipped' into their inversions by taking the top note(s) to the bottom or the bottom note(s) to the top. Different inversions often create quite different realizations of a chord sequence. In addition, chord tones can be divided between the hands in any number of different ways, and the rhythmic textures that can be used are practically infinite. Module Fourteen of the Musicarta Canon Project explores some of these possibilities.

Here is the module performance.

CPA_M14_01

New inversions of the Canon triads

Here is a demonstration that recaps how the triads we have been using up to now were put together, and shows how to make different inversions of the chords – to play in the left hand, for this module.

CPA_M14_02 | CPM_M14_02

Listen to the audio and watch the performance on MidiPiano. You see-and-hear eight sections.

Familiar material

1. The original string of thirds, here played top note in the right hand, bottom note in the left.

2. The third note of the triads.

3. These two put together to make triads, still split between the hands.

4. The triads played with just the right hand.

New material

5. The string of thirds, split between the hands, played an octave lower.

6. The same third note (to make the triad) as before, but now above the thirds, and played in the right hand.

7. These two put together to make new inversions of the triads, still split between the hands.

8. The new triads played in the left hand.

Without trying to play, read the list as you listen to the audio clip, matching the sections

114

as you hear them with the numbered items on the list. Then watch the MIDI performance on MidiPiano with the list in front of you so you can check you understand the 'which-hand-plays-what' descriptions of the eight sections.

Maximize your understanding by doing each of these tasks at least twice.

Now try to play the eight sections. If you play the MIDI file, either in MidiPiano or in Windows Media Player (or similar), you can slow down the performance and pause after each section to give yourself more time.

Voice movement diagrams

In the music, you see voice movement diagrams – the straight-and-sloping lines that show how the notes in the chords move. Study them closely. Compare the voice movement diagrams of the original (section 4) and new (section 8) strings of triads.

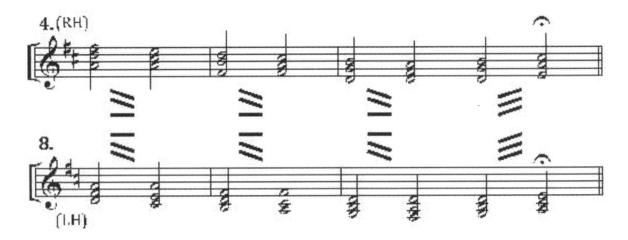

The note-that-stays-the-same (flat line) is now at the top instead of at the bottom . See if you can hear that in the audio file:

CPA_M14_03	CPM_M14_03

Watch the MIDI file in MidiPiano to clarify.

Finger the new string of triads sensibly, using fingers 2–4 and 3–5 to allow smooth movement in the pairs.

Playing a melodic variation by ear

Listen to this audio clip:

CPA_M14_04	CPM_M14_04

It's the new inversions of the first pair of chords in the Canon chord sequence (D and A) played in the left hand, with a simple melody fragment played in the right hand. The right hand plays the 'model' for the melodic Canon variation we are creating in this module.

You may be able to play the chords-plus-melody fragment straight off, or you may need to use the Module Thirteen 'contour' method to be able to play it. Read through the following instructions anyway – it will be your working method for more and more difficult challenges.

Establish the rhythmic profile

The rhythm is quite simple. Listen again and try to 'tap it out'. The left hand plays the first two triads from the new inverted string, one per (four-count) bar. What does the right hand do?

Here's the beat map for the fragment, which gives the melodic (RH) fragment rhythm:

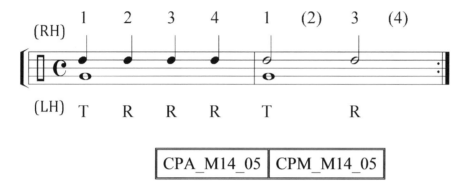

The audio of the beat map has a 'click track' to help you keep time. Jot down the right hand rhythm (four crotchets/quarter notes, two minims/half notes) on a piece of paper for the next stage.

Establish the melodic profile

Now listen to the audio clip again to identify the up/down/same melodic profile of the segment.

CPA_M14_04 | CPM_M14_04

Put arrows between the notes of your beat map, listening repeatedly to make sure you've got it right. Remember that the arrows don't have to show by how much the melody goes up or down.

Here's the 'answer':

Here's the audio again. Listen to it as you study the beat-map-with-arrows until you can see-and-hear how the two match up.

Attach the melodic profile to the actual chords

Now we know the rhythm and the melodic shape of the pattern, we have to 'attach' it to the first pair of chords – D major and A major – and find out which actual notes to play.

Melodies usually start on a chord tone (root, third or fifth). Listen to the audio of our fragment again and try the root, third and fifth of the D major chord (above the left hand chords) one after the other until you have decided which chord tone is the starting note.

Once you have found the starting point, following the up/down arrows (in steps to next-door D major scale tones) gives you the five of the pattern's six right hand notes.

The right hand starts on F sharp. Place notes according to the contour arrows as far as the first right hand note in the second bar.

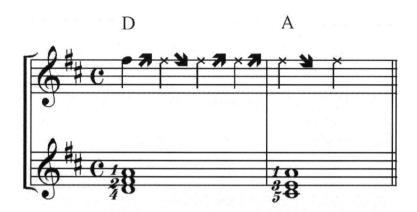

If you stick to scale degrees, following the arrows brings you to note A (a chord tone of A major, the next chord.) That would be logical!

The arrow between the last two right hand notes points down, and the last note is very probably going to be an A major chord tone, too – it would 'stick out' if it weren't. Which A major chord tone is the last note?

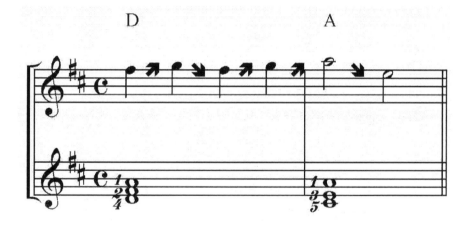

The pattern starts on the third of the D chord (note F sharp) and arrives on the root of the A chord (note A). Then it drops to the fifth of the A chord (note E).

Transferring the pattern to the other pairs of chords

As in Module Thirteen, you can use the regular structure of the Canon chord sequence to get a whole chorus out of the work you've just done. To make that work, you now have to strip out the actual chords and think in terms of 'any pair of chords'.

Here is the segment labelled that way:

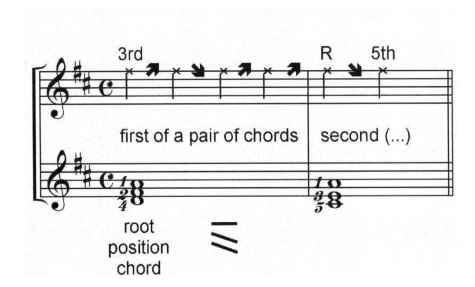

So, for the next two pairs of chords (the next four bars), the right hand will start on the third of B minor (note D), and on the third of G major (note B).

Here is the audio of the pattern in the next (second) pair of chords – B minor and F sharp minor.

CPA_M14_06

Here is the audio of the pattern in the third pair of chords – G and D major.

CPA_M14_07

From the beginning, the performance so far sounds like this:

CPA_M14_08

You hear in this audio how a bit of delay and anticipation naturally creeps in, making the riff sound quite 'pop-py'. If the clip sounds familiar, it's because the Canon chord sequence has been re-used countless times by songwriters and composers.

The last pair of chords

The melody for the last pair of chords starts the same way – from the third of G (note B). But following our up/down pattern doesn't get us to an A major chord tone in the final bar, but to note D – the fourth, counting up from A.

A suspension, in other words. The suspension can resolve simply to the third in the same rhythmic pattern as before:

CPA_M14_09

Note that if you have a suspension – note D – in the right hand, you can't play the full A chord in the left hand (because the D in the right hand would clash with the C sharp in the left hand) so you play just the outside notes of the left hand chord.

The melodic contour for that music is the same as for the first three pairs. Listen to the audio again and check.

Or you can be a bit more adventurous and fill the last bar with crotchets (quarter notes).

CPA_M14_10

The suspension resolves, then you climb back up to the starting note for the next chorus. The left hand walks up in tenths. Try to 'just think' the up/down arrows – for both left and right hands – into this last-pair beat map.

Playing the module performance

You now have all the components of the module performance.

CPA_M14_01	CPM_M14_01	CBT_D14

Note the drum track recommendation – loop it in Audacity to back your performance.

Listen out for these features to copy:

- The first chorus is played with some delayed and anticipated notes in the right hand. The left hand is played quite straight, apart from some repeated bass notes in the second half.

- In the second chorus, the notes of the left hand chords are broken up B M T, T M B. You will need to look at the fingering and play the descending T, M, B with fingers 1, 2, 4 to get it smooth.

- In the third chorus, the lowest note of the left hand chord bounces on beats 1 (2) & 3 (4) – a classic rock beat pattern. The ending is all D major chord tones with a typical ending rallentando ('slowing down', indicated 'Ral' in classical music).

Transposing challenge

Your module transposing challenge is to play the module performance in the keys of G and C. The more keys you play a chord sequence in, the more you see the pattern in it and the more able you are to 'just sit down and play'.

Here's the module performance in G.

CPA_M14_11	CPM_M14_11

To prepare, repeat the triad inversion process in G.

CPA_M14_12	CPM_M14_12

Here is the G major transposing table:

Key: D	D	Em	F♯m	G	A	Bm	C♯dim
RNS	I	ii	iii	IV	V	vi	vii°
Key: G	G	Am	Bm	C	D	Em	F♯dim

You remember that in the Roman numeral system, the Canon chord sequence is:

Canon (RNS)	I	V	vi	iii	IV	I	IV	V

Transpose the module performance into C as well.

CPA_M14_13	CPM_M14_13

Prepare by repeating the triad inversion process in C.

CPA_M14_14	CPM_M14_14

Here is the C major transposing table:

Key: D	D	Em	F♯m	G	A	Bm	C♯dim
RNS	I	ii	iii	IV	V	vi	vii°
Key: C	C	Dm	Em	F	G	Am	Bdim

Remember, in the Roman numeral system, the Canon chord sequence is:

Canon (RNS)	I	V	vi	iii	IV	I	IV	V

Keep in mind the 'contour' features of the 2-bar melodic model – its shape and what chord tone it starts on. The melodic fragment we're modelling:

- Starts on the third of the first chord in a pair.

- Follows this contour:

- It arrives on the root of the second chord of the pair, and then
- Drops to the fifth of the second chord (first three pairs only).

This module represents a great deal of work and a high level of accomplishment, but the tasks set are achievable because they build on what you already know. Nevertheless, you should expect to come back to this module many times before you can 'just do it'. Working through this material one more time will never be time wasted.

EAR TRAINING AND HARMONIC VARIATION

A few gifted keyboard players can just sit down and play what they hear – either in their heads or from a CD – but most musicians have to take a more methodical approach to developing this seemingly magical ability. Your in-depth familiarity with the Canon chord sequence provides a great opportunity to develop your 'playing-by-ear' skills.

You need to be able to say and play the Canon chord sequence – roots and triads – well. Revise the chord sequence.

‖:D	A	Bm	F♯m	G	D	G	A :‖

Preparation

Play-and-say the original Canon chord sequence (usual triad string, roots in bass) in two places. Repeat.

CPA_M15_01		CPA_M15_02

If the bass note is the root, and you can identify the bass note, you will usually have got the chord. 'Sing' the chords to the bass line. It doesn't matter how good you are at singing, or even whether you sing in tune; making the effort is instructional in itself.

CPA_M15_03

Name the chords in the following audio files. They are the 'usual string' Canon triads, but not in the order they normally occur. You don't have to play the chord or get the top note – just say which of the Canon chords it is. (If you can name the bass note, you can name the chord.)

The first set of chords starts and ends on D. The chord is played once, then played a second time and named. There are five sets.

CPA_M15_04

The second set of chords does not necessarily start on D.

CPA_M15_05

The same exercise with the chords an octave lower.

CPA_M15_06

Identifying the melody note

The chord sequence in the next set of audio files is always the standard Canon sequence and the bass note is always the root, but the right hand plays inversions of the Canon chord sequence triads. Identify the highest note and play the right hand inversion of the standard Canon chord sequence chord which has that note at the top. The top note always moves the smallest distance possible between chords.

Make notes using a table like the one suggested in Module Nine (example only).

Top note	f sharp	e	d	c sharp	b	a	b	c sharp
Chord	D	A	Bm	F#m	G	D	G	A

CPA_M15_07	CPA_M15_08
CPA_M15_09	CPA_M15_10
CPA_M15_11	CPA_M15_12
CPM_M15_07 to 12	

You can check your answers using the MIDI file. Playing along with the MidiPiano performance is a good up-to-speed exercise.

RH inversions with 'slash chord' basses

These again are the standard Canon chord sequence but with varying RH inversions over the 'slash bass' bass line. Identify the top note.

CPA_M15_13	CPA_M15_14
CPA_M15_15	CPA_M15_16
CPA_M15_17	CPA_M15_18
CPM_M15_13 to 18	

Harmonic variations in Canon recordings

In the great wash of instrument parts in the Canon, the F sharp minor chord sometimes becomes a D major 'slash chord' – D major with F sharp in the bass (D/F#).

Similarly the second G chord sometimes gets note E at the top and becomes an E minor slash chord Em/G – E minor with G in the bass. E minor is the only chord in the key of D major that doesn't appear in the original chord sequence, so this 'completes the set'.

Incorporating both variations, you might have something like this:

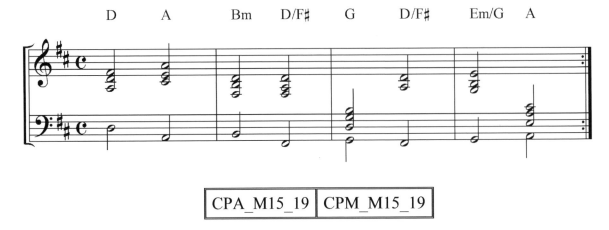

CPA_M15_19	CPM_M15_19

(The chords are written as minims, but that doesn't mean the music is any faster.)

This chord sequence might be 'realised' (brought to life) like this.

CPA_M15_20	CPM_M15_20	CBT_D15

Real riffs

You were promised earlier that studying the Canon chord sequence in depth would help you play lots of other music. Here are four 'real riffs' such as you might hear on a CD and want to play. They all use only the Canon chords, though not always in the exact same order.

CPA_M15_21	CPM_M15_21	CBT_D16

This riff uses the Canon sequence as far as the G chord, then reverses along the chord sequence back to the start. The chords are played 'plain' first. Be satisfied with something close to the actual syncopation in the recorded riff. The point is to 'have a go' and get a riff of your own out of the exercise.

CPA_M15_22	CPM_M15_22	CBT_D17

Another reversal, but this time only as far as B minor, then with extra material.

| CPA_M15_23 | CPM_M15_23 | CBT_D15 |

A 'slash chord' pure Canon sequence. Getting the top notes of the RH inversions (two choruses) is essential.

Music is often made more interesting by stretching phrases. We expect music to come in four-bar or eight-bar phrases, so an unexpected 'extension' keeps the interest up. Here is the previous variation with a two-chord extension made by 'slipping in' chords Em/G and F♯m/A in bars 7 and 8 to make a 10-bar phrase.

| CPA_M15_24 | CPM_M15_24 |

| CPA_M15_25 | CPM_M15_25 | CBT_D06 |

A typical song chorus chord sequence made of Canon chords, but in a different order.

When you're trying to work out a song from a CD, you have to train yourself to listen through the fancy surface to the chords beneath. This is the background – the supporting chords – you should hear:

| CPA_M15_26 |

Only afterwards do you put in the rhythm, fills and melody.

| CPA_M15_27 | CPM_M15_27 | CBT_D18 |

This riff breaks the eight right hand quavers of the bar up into groups of three, three, and two (3+3+2) – a classic pop/rock quaver grouping.

The broken chord pattern is this:

cT   B   M   T   M   B   ?   ?B

The two question marks stand for 'wildcards' – usually next-door notes connecting the top note of the bar smoothly and pleasantly to the top note of the next bar.

As with the previous riff, you want first to listen through the texture to the chords and learn those before you even attempt the broken chord pattern and the connecting notes. Trying to work out all three things at the same time is not a good idea.

Here are the underlying chords you should hear:

CPA_M15_28	CPM_M15_28

This module is chiefly about training yourself to hear chords, but you will probably want to play the 'real life' riffs offered above.

They all have MIDI demonstration files, so you can crib the actual notes by sight if you can't get them by ear. Also, load the drum backing tracks into Audacity and get them looping with shift+spacebar, then see if you can work up your own riffs a bit like what you hear. Developing your own keyboard style and material is much more satisfying than learning to play someone else's performances.

The 'Canon Diaries' series of Mister Musicarta YouTube videos presents more ongoing explorations of the Canon chord sequence. see the Supplement at the end of the book.

FURTHER HARMONIC VARIATIONS

Knowing one single chord sequence – especially the Canon – and one key really well, opens the door to great creative freedom. This module contains a number of examples of the kind of experimentation you could be capable of if you continue to work on the Canon chord sequence the Musicarta way.

AABA form

The Canon cycles through the same simple eight-chord sequence numerous times, and relies on layering up instruments and melodic lines for its attraction. Then it ends, again very simply.

Most songs, though, aren't quite so simple. They often have an additional, different bit of material, slotted into the repeating 'same' section. Very often, the different section is slotted in third in a set of four phrases, giving what is called 'AABA form'.

Note that 'A' and 'B' have nothing to do with keys, chords or notes. They simply indicate that the three 'A' sections are the same or similar, while the 'B' section is different.

Here are some possible 'B' sections which could slot in to three 'A' sections to make a 32-bar 'AABA' song or piece.

Here is a Canon-based AABA chord sequence which uses only the familiar Canon chords.

CPA_M16_01	CPM_M16_01	CBT_D19

Here is the chord sequence.

D	A/C♯	Bm	F♯m/A	G	D/F♯	G	A(s–r)
D	A/C♯	Bm	F♯m/A	G	D/F♯	G	A
G	D/F♯	G	A	G	D/F♯	G	A
D	A/C♯	Bm	F♯m/A	G	D/F♯	G	A
D	G :A	D	D				

Examine the chord sequence. Note that the first, second and fourth lines are the same, and the third line is different – AABA form. The fifth line of the sequence is an extended ending. The abbreviation (s–r) stands for suspension–resolution. The chord symbol G :A in the fifth line indicates that the four counts in that bar are split between those two chords. (This is a universal convention.)

Here is the same performance with another possible B section:

CPA_M16_02	CPM_M16_02

Here is the chord sequence:

D	A/C♯	Bm	F♯m/A	G	D/F♯	G	A(s–r)
D	A/C♯	Bm	F♯m/A	G	D/F♯	G	A
F♯/A♯	Bm	A/C♯	D	Em/G		A7(s–r)	
D	A/C♯	Bm	F♯m/A	G	D/F♯	G	A
D	G :A	D	D				

Notice the F♯/A♯ slash chord in the new B section (third line of the sequence) The F♯ chord in the Canon is usually a minor chord – F♯m. There is no 'm' here, so the chord has to be major, and the third, note A, will be sharpened. This is the A♯ you play in the bass.

Mediant substitution

Mediant substitution is a powerful way of getting more out of any chord sequence.

The 'mediant' chord in a key is the chord built on the third note of the scale up from the tonic – the F sharp minor chord in the key of D. The 'submediant' chord in a key is the chord built on the note a third down from the tonic (the sixth scale degree) – B minor in key D.

Mediant substitution involves shifting the root and/or the chord up or down a third to generate rich new harmonies. This usually creates a seventh chord.

Play the first four chords of the Canon, then lower the roots a third and play them again. You get this:

CPA_M16_03	CPM_M16_03

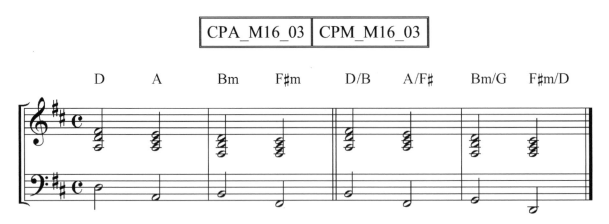

Immediately the chords sound a lot more modern. You can hear the potential of the chord sequence:

The slash-chord names of the altered chords in the music example above are not proper names – they just describe how the chords have been put together. Here is the same music with the chords named correctly:

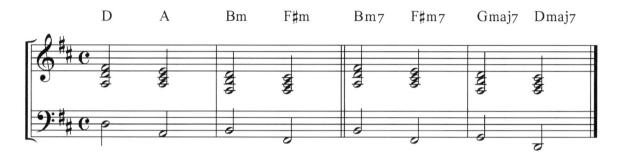

(You can learn all about <u>seventh chords</u> on the Musicarta site.)

Follow the same procedure with the last four chords in the chord sequence. You play the same chords in the right hand but lower the bass line a third. The original chords here get too low for this treatment, so inversions have been used.

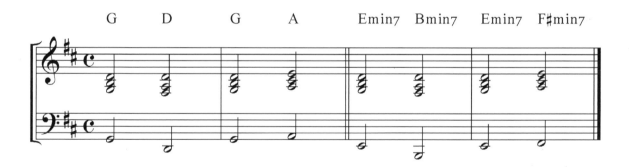

The complete bass mediant substitution chord sequence follows.

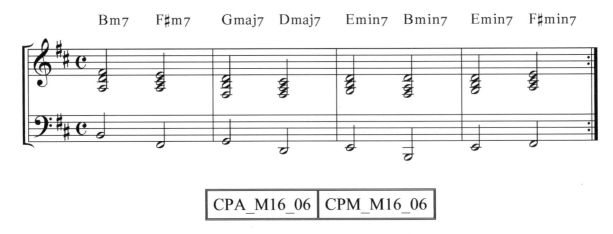

CPA_M16_06	CPM_M16_06

Here's a possible rendition in slow jazz waltz rhythm.

CPA_M16_07	CPM_M16_07	CBT_D09

The entire chord sequence has moved into a modal relative minor. Explore the <u>Modes Workbook</u> on the Musicarta site if you find these harmonies attractive.

Note: Some music theory texts distinguish between mediant and submediant substitution. Musicarta has not done so in this section. Experiment with keeping the bass the same and changing the right hand chord to the 'third up' substitute chord.

Fourths overlapping by only one tone

The three pairs of chords in the Canon chord sequence overlap by one scale degree. You will recognise the familiar bass line shape:

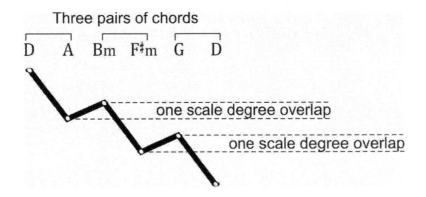

We can generate interesting chord sequences by having three pairs of chords the same size (i.e. roots still dropping a fourth) spaced one whole tone apart:

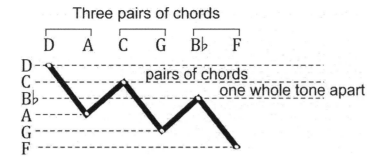

Listen to the two versions:

CPA_M16_08	CPM_M16_08

The 'whole tone apart' version is a lot more rock-sounding. Note that it takes us well outside the D major scale (C natural, F natural, B flat), and that all the chords are major.

Here's a riff based on this 'whole tone apart' chord sequence. 'Build-up' suggestions follow.

CPA_M16_09	CPM_M16_09	CBT_D10

Here's the chord sequence:

D	A	C	G	B♭	F	G	A
D	A	C	G	B♭	C	D	D
B♭	C	D	D	B♭	C	D	D

Everything, as far as possible, is in whole-tone steps: F – G – A at the end of the first half, B♭ – C – D at the end of the second half (and repeated).

When you hear a 'busy' riff like this that you might like to play, the first thing you do is try to listen through to the underlying chords. Here they are:

CPA_M16_10	CPM_M16_10

Of course, you want to know what the top note of the right hand chord is. The top note is easiest to hear. This musical shorthand is as good as written-out music:

Top note:	f♯	e	e	d	d	c	d	e
Chord:	D	A	C	G	B♭	F	G	A
	f♯	e	e	d	d	d	d	
	D	A	C	G	B♭	C	D	

133

The riff above demonstrates all the chord changes in as short a time as possible – as do most of the Musicarta Canon Project riffs. You don't have to play all the chords, or change quite so quickly. Just the first two pairs – chords D, A, C and G – are ample for a basic song sequence:

| CPA_M16_11 | CBT_D11 |

Here's the chord sequence used:

cD   A   C   G   D   A   C   G   A   C :G B

Try transposing the riff using chords C – G – B♭ – F, or G – D – F – C. The formula is:

- Two pairs of chords, the second pair a whole tone below the first.
- In each pair, both chords are major and the root falls a fourth.

Often, in the act of transposing, the keys feel different under your fingers and you stumble upon a slightly different version. This is often how musical creation takes place, so seize your variations boldly and 'lock them in'! Make a quick recording or jot down a musical shorthand version, then come back to them and work them up into your own piece or song.

This is the last module in the Musicarta Canon Project.

Looking forward, you are now in a position to use your in-depth knowledge of the Canon's seminal chord sequence as a springboard for developing your musical understanding and skills.

For example, your familiarity with the Canon chord sequence offers a significant opportunity to improve your aural skills, and know just by listening what chords are being used in a song. Your repeated, focussed listening to the Canon chord sequence provides a solid foundation for the 'educated guesswork' that underpins this seemingly magical skill.

Most mainstream pop/rock songs don't stray far from the chords that are natural to their key, like the Canon chords in D major (with the addition of E minor, as discussed in Module Fifteen). Listen to the 'golden oldies' shows on your radio, or to your 60s/70s/80s Greatest Hits compilations and ask yourself, "If this song was in D (like the Canon), what would that chord be?"

Transposing is key to musical creativity. Keep going back to the Roman numeral system of naming chords until it becomes second nature. Play the Canon chord sequence (the 'usual string of triads') in five different keys every day. Use inversions in the right hand to make top-note tunes, and transpose again. Transpose the harmonic variations in this Module Fifteen and Sixteen into other keys.

In the end, though, nothing beats just 'messing around'. Learners find it hard to accept that they can, in fact, 'just sit down and play'. Often, this is a matter of unrealistic expectations – of expecting to improvise something perfect, out of the blue, first time off.

More often, however, what you create is based on something you already know – the Canon chord sequence, for example, plain or altered – and is a performance built from repeated not-quite-there-yet attempts, probably with some aids-to-memory jotted down along the way. As a start, you can play the Canon chord sequence using a keyboard texture and rhythm copied from another piece or song. Or just loop up a drum track and see what comes up!

See the Canon diaries Supplement at the end of this volume for more Canon-based explorations.

There's lots more chord-based creativity material at musicarta.com. Like the Canon Project, the Pyramids Variations series builds an impressive performance from simple keyboard resources, teaching theory basics along the way. The Pyramids series also goes on to create variations on its chord sequence – the best way to develop creativity.

The Chord Progressions series at musicarta.com builds chord fluency by introducing the key chords one at a time, starting with the famous 'One, Four, Five' trio of chords – the basis of vast amounts of popular music, while the Modes series explores how this pre-modern key system can still generate attractively-different chord sequences.

Both the Pyramids Variations and Musicarta Key Chords Volume 1 are available as full digital home-study downloads, and as print-on-demand titles at Amazon Books.

The Musicarta Pentatonics material teaches these invaluable scales, which are ready-made for improvising, while the Blues and 12-Bar tab will teach you the basics of boogie in no time. There is also material in the Beat and Rhythm section to progressively improve your ability to play complicated off-the-beat music, an essential skill in modern keyboard work.

Make musicarta.com your springboard to keyboard creativity! Have a Musicarta project 'on the go' at all times. Your expanding knowledge and educated musical ear will help you listen to your favourite music with an "I can do that!" attitude. Above all, play constructively every day. In music, as elsewhere, persistence pays dividends, and there is hardly anything you can't achieve with steady work – and Musicarta!

ANSWERS TO MODULE CHALLENGES

This section contains the written-out music and MIDI reference numbers for the various challenges in the Canon Project modules.

Module One

Further variations Type One: Fewer notes

This is the same as the last variation you played, but the second right hand note is tied to the first – it doesn't sound separately.

| CPA_M1_08 | CPM_M1_08 |

Type Two: More notes

This version still uses the same notes, but changes more often:

| CPA_M1_09 | CPM_M1_09 |

Module Two

Here is the written-out music for the two Module Two audio challenge variations, which combine the bass line with the thirds from Module One in the right hand. The MIDI performance file numbers are right underneath each example.

| CPA_M2_13 | CPM_M2_13 |

| CPA_M2_14 | CPM_M2_14 |

Module Three

Here is the written-out music and the MIDI file reference number for the Module Three audio challenge.

CPA_M3_14	CPM_M3_14

Module Four

Here is the written-out music for the Module Four audio challenge. The MIDI file reference is in the table beneath. Listen to the audio as you read the music to build your ability to read.

| CPA_M5_15 | CPM_M5_15 |

Module Five

BMT texture challenge

Here is the broken chord 'recipe' as a music sketch, and played out again.

| CPA_M5_06 | CPM_M5_06 |

Module Five: BMT texture with thirds

Combine thirds with a broken chord texture. Use the last BMT pattern again:

‖T B M T |T B M T :‖

but play thirds where it says 'T' instead of a single top note. Play the pattern over the 'bouncing' bass line from Module Four.

| CPA_M5_11 | CPM_M5_11 |

Module Six

Canon broken chord study

| CPA_M6_23 | CPM_M6_23 |

Module Eight

Here is the written-out music for the Module Eight audio challenge.

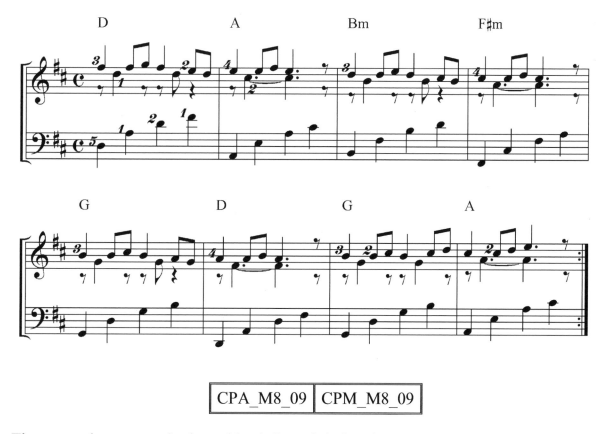

| CPA_M8_09 | CPM_M8_09 |

The stems-down notes in the treble clef are right hand notes too – they are the 'sticky' notes.

Module Ten

Audio challenge

Here is the written-out music and MIDI performance file of the Module Ten audio challenge performance with the added 'in-between notes' in the even-numbered bars.

Complete the chord sequence using the suggested accompaniment pattern.

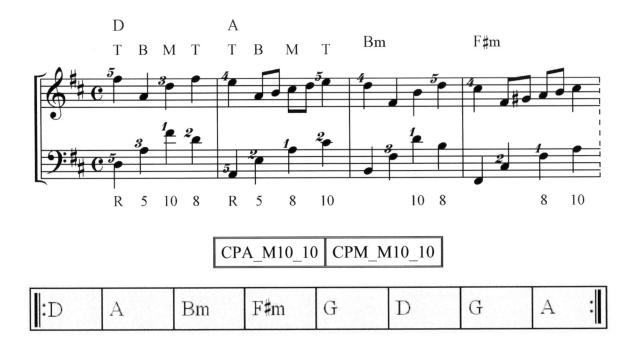

Mixed-type accompaniments challenge

Your challenge was to select what accompaniment goes best with given right hand patterns. Here are some suggestions.

The two-chorus example:

CPA_M10_14 | CPM_M10_14

Here's a suggestion for the next example:

(simile - two-bar pattern, repeating)

CPA_M10_15	CPM_M10_15

For the T M B T |T M B T broken chord pattern, try R, 5, 10, 8 right the way through ('*simile*').

CPA_M10_16 | CPM_M10_16

Accompaniment table challenge

Here is the written-out music of the Module Ten mixed-type two-handed accompaniment in the table

CPA_M10_17	CPM_M10_17

Chord	D	A	Bm	F#m	G	D
Hands	L R R R	L R R R	(always L R R R)			
Chord-tone	R 10 5 8	R 5 8 10	R 10 5 8	R 5 8 10	(two-bar repeating)	

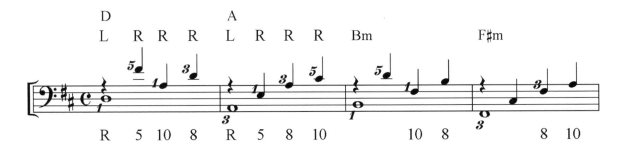

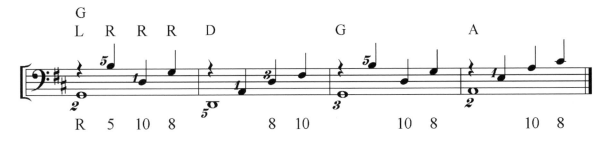

Module Eleven

The suspension riff

Here is the music for the build-up to the Module Eleven sample suspensions riff.

CPA_M11_12 | CPM_M11_12

149

Where the syncopation starts, you see the counts written in and together, left, right (TLR) analysis. By all means, just 'have a go', but meticulous counting and TLR analysis are the methodical way to build two-handed syncopation skills.

Remember that both Widows Media Player and MidiPiano can be set to repeat (and slow down) the performance files, giving you lots of time to learn the riffs by simply copying.

Back to Module Eleven

Transposing challenge

Here is the music for the Module Eleven suspensions in F transposing challenge. Copy the left hand in-between notes and syncopation from the audio.

Module Twelve

Here is the music for the Module Twelve broken-chord-over-slash-bass variation.

| CPA_M12_05 | CPM_M12_05 |

Watch the performance on MidiPiano using the MIDI file referenced in the table.

Module Thirteen

Audio challenge: First chorus | CPM_M13_10 |

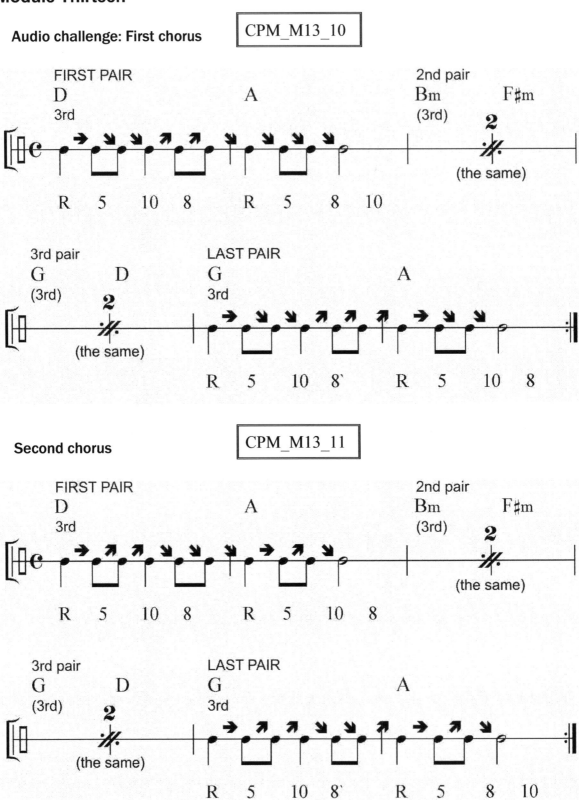

Second chorus | CPM_M13_11 |

Scale practice patterns

Here is the written-out music for the two scale practice patterns presented as line diagrams only in the Key of D Major supplement.

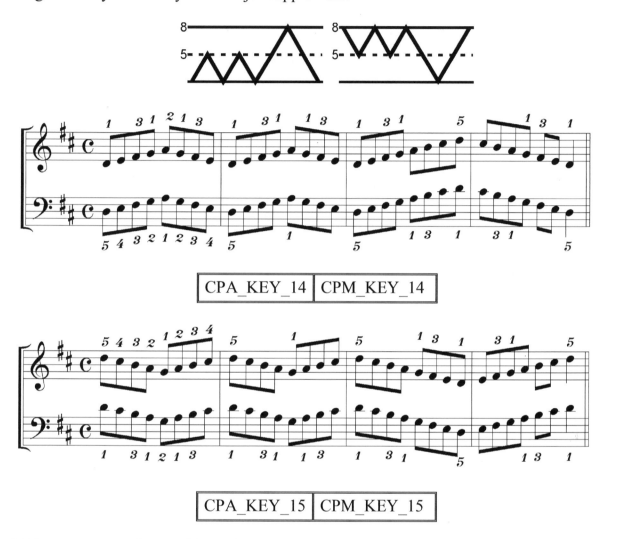

| CPA_KEY_14 | CPM_KEY_14 |

| CPA_KEY_15 | CPM_KEY_15 |

Make sure you understand how the line diagram represents the practice pattern.

THE KEY OF D MAJOR

> **NOTE:** The first part of this module repeats the Key of D Major material in the Preparing to Learn section at the start of this volume. Revise if necessary. The <u>scale practice patterns</u> start just below.

Pachelbel's Canon is in the key of D major. You need to use black keys F sharp and C sharp to make music in D sound right.

The black keys necessary for playing 'in a key' are indicated in the key signature.

In D, all notes written on the lines or in the spaces shaded in the diagram above (any F or C, in fact) are played on black keys F sharp and C sharp, which replace white keys F and C.

This diagram shows one octave of D major scale-tones. It could be anywhere on the keyboard.

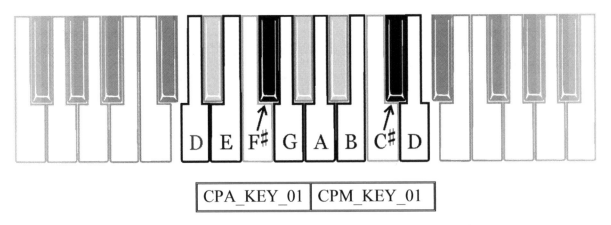

The replaced white keys F and C have been greyed out, along with the black keys you do not use. This is how the well-schooled keyboard player sees the keyboard as soon as he or she sees the two-sharp key signature.

(Note that, if a key signature shows two sharps, they are always F sharp and C sharp.)

D major scale fingering

It is usual, in keyboard playing, to learn keys by learning the scales. If you know your D major scale, you know all the basic notes used in the key of D major – and all the notes in the Canon. You know what the key of D major 'looks like', and you will be much less likely to play wrong notes. You will learn the Canon much more quickly and enjoy playing more if you do the ground work of learning and playing the D major scale.

Here is our sample octave of D major showing which fingers play which notes. (Use keys in the middle of your keyboard if you want to experiment.)

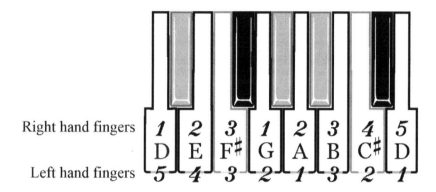

There are eight notes in the octave but only five fingers on the hand, so we have to play a group of three fingers as well as the handful of five:

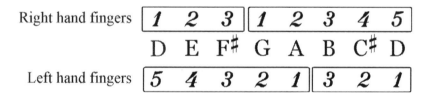

This means you have to pass the thumb under or the third finger over to play the full octave.

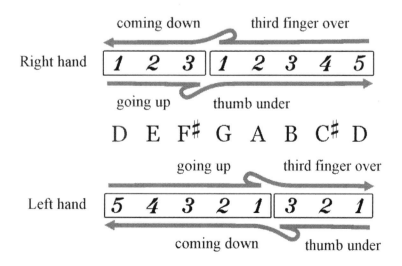

155

In the scale practice patterns that follow, you will use these piano keys and fingers, around middle C.

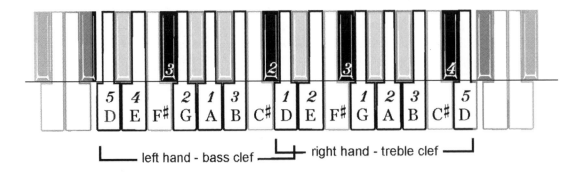

Scale practice patterns

The thumb-under movement, hands separately

Practise the right hand thumb-under movement three times, then complete the octave.

| CPA_KEY_04 | CPM_M1_04 |

Revise the left hand thumb-under movement in the same way. You will play from the top.

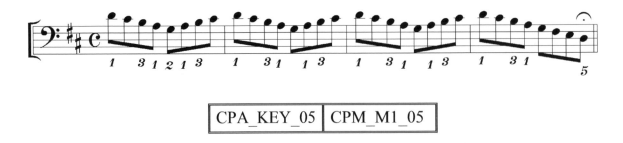

| CPA_KEY_05 | CPM_M1_05 |

Thumb under, hands together

The main challenge when playing scales with both hands together is that there is a third-finger-over or thumb-under movement in one hand while the other hand is playing simple 1–2–3–4–5 or 5–4–3–2–1.

This is something that needs practice. Here is a study for this challenging movement.

| CPA_KEY_06 | CPM_M1_06 |

You run up and down the first five notes of the D major scale, hands together, using the actual scale fingering. The right hand practices the thumb-under and third-finger-over movement (complicated) while the left hand just plays from one side of the hand to the other (simple).

Note: You can practise the right hand on its own first if you need to.

The thumb-under/third-finger-over movements are still boxed, but the black key F sharp is not circled. Both third fingers play an F sharp.

Practice until the fingering is 'in your hand'.

Next, we use a similar study for the top five notes of the scale, where the left hand does the 'complicated' movement and the right hand is 'simple'.

| CPA_KEY_07 | CPM_M1_07 |

The black key in this part of the scale is C sharp – right hand finger 4 (RH4) and left hand finger 2 (LH2).

(As before, you can practise your left hand on its own first if you need to.)

Rehearse thumb under, then all the way

Rehearse the first five fingers, then run up to the top of the octave. You will run out of left hand fingers – this is where you bring your third finger over.

Play from the bottom first.

| CPA_KEY_08 | CPM_KEY_08 |

Practise the pattern from the top down as well.

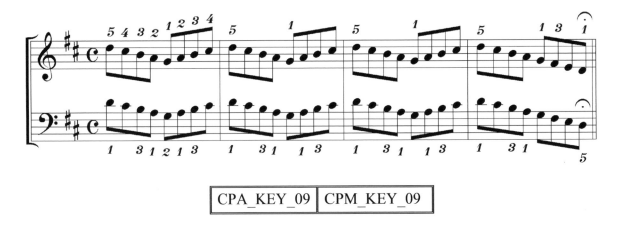

| CPA_KEY_09 | CPM_KEY_09 |

One octave hands together

You have rehearsed the thumb-under component of the one-octave scales. Now play one-octave scales, hands together, from the bottom to the top.

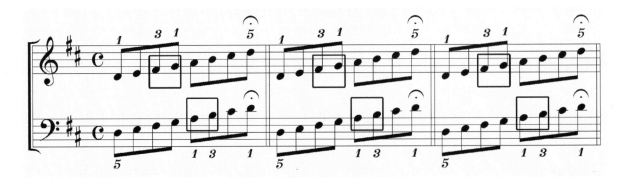

| CPA_KEY_10 | CPM_KEY_10 |

Stop at the top briefly before playing again.

Play from the top down.

| CPA_KEY_11 | CPM_KEY_11 |

Play one octave up-and-then-down.

| CPA_KEY_12 | CPM_KEY_12 |

Play one octave down-and-then-up.

| CPA_KEY_13 | CPM_KEY_13 |

Revise your motivation for learning scales

All music is in a certain key. (The Canon is 'in D major'.) On the piano keyboard, this means using some of the black piano keys instead of some of the white piano keys. These black keys are indicated in the key signature at the start of a line of keyboard music

To play the pieces or songs you want, you will need to be able to play in several keys – certainly C, G, D, A, and E majors (the 'sharp' keys), and also in F, B flat and E flat (the 'flat' keys).

Playing scales is a tried-and-tested way of learning keys – avoiding the 'wrong note' white piano keys and playing the right black keys instead. Learning scales is not a 'jumping through the hoops' task – it's about becoming a better musician.

Top musicians can play the notes on their chosen instrument quickly, one after another. Practising scales and finger exercises – a lot – is the only way of acquiring this finger dexterity. Do it for yourself – be strict, and put the hours in early on in your musical career, if you can.

Playing scale practice patterns by shape

The idea behind scale practice for the modern popular music keyboard player is the get the keys into the fingers, and the less written music involved, the better. It is therefore a good idea to learn to practice scales from scale practice pattern 'shapes', rather than from notes.

Look at this scale practice pattern (which you have already played):

| CPA_KEY_08 | CPM_KEY_08 |

It could be represented by this line diagram:

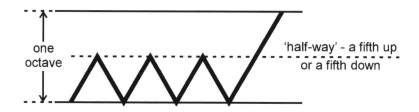

The pattern runs up and down the first five notes three times, then all the way to the top. Play the audio and/or the MIDI file to see how the line diagram represents the pattern.

The next practice pattern does the same thing, but upside down – from the top.

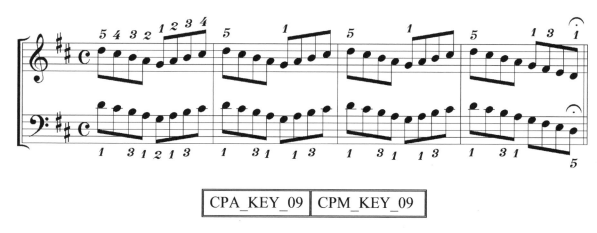

| CPA_KEY_09 | CPM_KEY_09 |

As a line diagram, it will look like this:

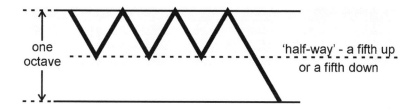

Play the audio and/or the MIDI file to see how the line diagram represents the pattern.

Other scale practice shapes

As line diagrams, other scale practice patterns you have encountered in this module so far will look like this:

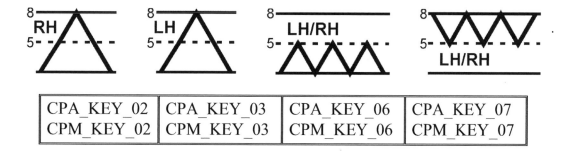

| CPA_KEY_02 | CPA_KEY_03 | CPA_KEY_06 | CPA_KEY_07 |
| CPM_KEY_02 | CPM_KEY_03 | CPM_KEY_06 | CPM_KEY_07 |

RH and LH mean 'Play with the right hand (or left hand) alone'. LH/RH means 'Play with hands together'.

Play the scale practice patterns in D major from the line diagrams alone. You yourself have to remember two things:

- The black keys, F sharp and C sharp, and
- The scale fingering – where the thumb passes under or the third finger over, in each hand.

Check, using the audio and MIDI performance files, that you have got it right. If necessary, scroll back and check the scale practice patterns music.

Here is the next set of scale practice patterns:

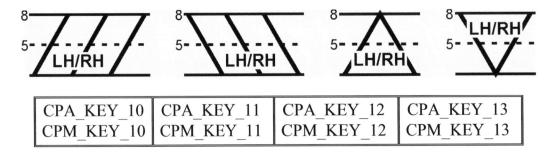

| CPA_KEY_10 | CPA_KEY_11 | CPA_KEY_12 | CPA_KEY_13 |
| CPM_KEY_10 | CPM_KEY_11 | CPM_KEY_12 | CPM_KEY_13 |

You want to be 'seeing the key of D in the keyboard' – no white key F's of C's, but black-key F sharps and C sharps instead. Here's the 'virtual D' keyboard again:

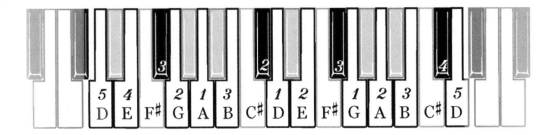

Check your scale fingering

If you're working on your own, only you can say if you're using the right fingers or not. You know you've gone wrong with the fingering somewhere if you:

- Run out of fingers with notes of the scale still left to play, or
- End up with fingers to spare (that is, not on finger 5 or 1), or
- Find you're trying to play a black key with the thumb.

If that is the case:

- Back-track until you identify your mistake – so you can correct it.

- Practice the right way at least twice as many times as you played it wrong, to correct your muscle memory.

Collected scale practice pattern shapes

Here are the collected scale practice pattern shapes. RH and LH mean 'Play with the right hand (or left hand) alone'. LH?RH means 'Play with hands together'.

Playing the D major scale from these patterns will reinforce your knowledge of the key of D major and improve your progress through the Canon Project modules. It will also improve your ability to see shape and pattern in music generally.

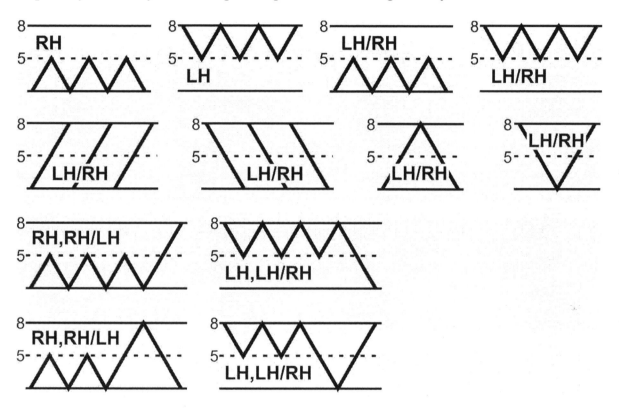

Scale pattern challenge

You haven't seen the last two patterns in the collection before. Study them carefully, then try playing them, hands separately and together, from just the line diagram: The written out music is in the 'Answers' section.

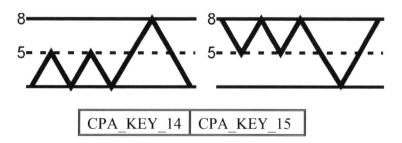

| CPA_KEY_14 | CPA_KEY_15 |

| CPM_KEY_14 | CPM_KEY_15 |

You can use scale practice patterns like these to practice any major or minor scale. Getting away from written-out scale music will improve the value of your scale practice many-fold. The D major fingering you have learned works for C major and the sharp keys G, D, A and E. All you have to do is start on the tonic (the name-note of the scale), and substitute black keys for white keys as shown in the key signature.

MAJOR AND MINOR CHORDS

The Canon chord sequence presents a great opportunity to discover the difference between major and minor chords.

Telling the difference between major and minor chords is easiest if we use root position triads, as for the inversions drills in Module Six.

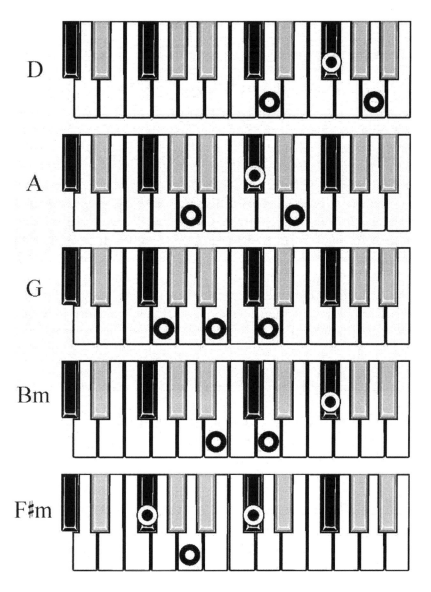

The three major chords have been grouped together, followed by the two minor chords below.

Note first that chord symbols take it for granted that a chord is major. 'D' means D major. You do have to specify if it's a minor chord by putting the lower case 'm' right after the capital-letter chord symbol – Bm (B minor), or F♯m (F sharp minor), for example. Also, you don't have to say "major" – except to avoid ambiguity. "D" (the chord) means D major.

Telling major and minor chords by sound

Here are the chords in the table above played from the top of the table down.

> CPA_MM_01

There are two differences in the chords. The first is pitch – how high or lower the chords are. This is not what we are interested in here. The second is tonality – the first three chords are major, the second two are minor.

Can you tell whether each of the five chords is major or minor just by how it sounds? People often say that the major chord has a 'happy' sound, and the minor chord, 'sad'.

Here are the chords again with their major/minor quality specified.

> CPA_MM_02

This might still not be clear, because the chords are higher or lower and this confuses the issue. Here are the chords again, this time, each one changed into its opposite quality. then back.

> CPA_MM_03

Major and minor – telling by counting

All the triads in the audio clips are root position (PMPMP) triads, but still some are major and some are minor. In order to see why, we have to count semitones, not just scale tones. This method is easiest with root position triads – this is one of the reasons for practicing the inversions-to-root-position operations in Module Six.

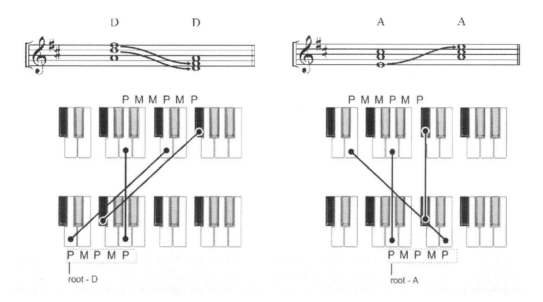

Two things to note before we start.

1. We start counting semitones from zero, the same way as we use a ruler.

2. The numbers in the following apply to major and minor triads in root position only.

The first thing we notice is that all the pairs of outside notes are seven semitones apart – so that's not what makes them different.

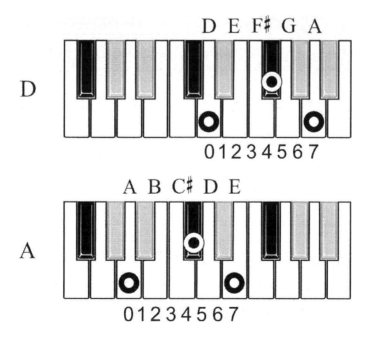

Count the semitones in the rest of the outside pairs to check this.

This seven-semitone distance is properly called 'a perfect fifth'. For now, we can say just 'a fifth'. Count the scale tones or note letter names to check – you will find there are five (see illustration). Remember that when we count 'intervals' like a fifth or a third, we start counting scale tones from 'one' – there is no zero. When we count semitones, however, we do start from zero, as on a ruler.

The difference between root position major and minor triads is whether the middle note is closer to the bottom note (the root) or closer to the top.

In root position major triads, the middle note is closer to the top. In minor triads, it's closer to the bottom.

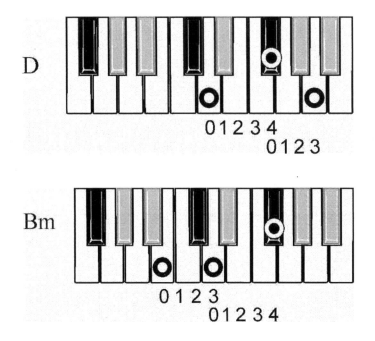

The difference is only one semitone. Count the semitones in the other major and minor chords to make sure you understand.

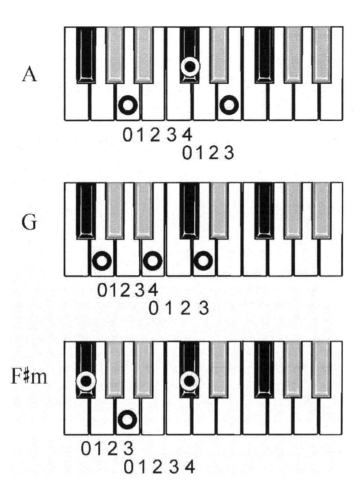

The major/minor rule

The rule is this:

- In a root position major chord, the third (middle note of a root position triad) is four semitones (two whole tones) above the root. This interval (distance) is called a 'major third'. The middle note is closer to the top than to the bottom of the triad.

- In a root position minor chord, the third is only three semitones (one-and-a-half whole tones) above the root. This interval is called a 'minor third'. The middle note is closer to the bottom than to the top of the triad.

Chords have to be in root (PMPMP) position to use the semitone counting method given here.

Changing chords from major to minor and vice versa

You can make minor chords out of the Canon major chords and vice versa just by sliding the third (the middle note of the PMPMP chord) a semitone up or down. Study the following table and copy the audio files for practice forming major and minor triads. Watch the MIDI file performance on MidiPiano for more guidance.

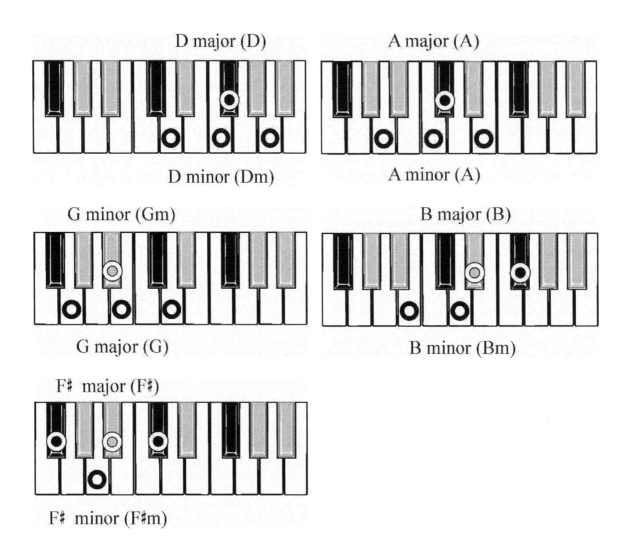

CPA_MM_04

The audio and MIDI performance files for the table above play major, minor, major chords for D, A and G (twice each), then minor, major, minor chords for B minor and F sharp minor.

Play around with major-minor chord difference. Learn to build major and minor chords on any root – and invert them.

Note that 'major' and 'minor' have nothing to do with black keys and white keys, as pupils sometimes think. The third in a chord – the note that makes it either major or minor – is equally likely to be a black or white key.

Check out www.musicarta.com for more chords resources via the site navbar 'Chords' tab.

THE MUSICARTA CANON PROJECT
ACCOMPANIMENT PRACTICE PATTERNS

Dozens of accompaniment patterns can be built from the root, fifth, octave and third of a chord, and time spent 'getting your fingers round' these notes can never be wasted.

These practice patterns form part of your Module Eight work – see the module for an explanation.

Your two fundamental tasks are:

1. To know without hesitation what the root, fifth, octave and tenth of the five Canon chords are , and

2. To develop a balanced hand position and the muscle memory needed to get to the notes.

Expect to find this practicing quite tiring. Don't overdo it – rest your hand and arm, and shake out the tension before resuming.

The practice patterns have a definite rhythm, which you should listen out for. The six-eight meter (rhythm) is usually counted "**One**-and-a **Two**-and-a", and having this count going on in the back of your mind will help you get better at 'keeping the notes coming'.

The practice patterns

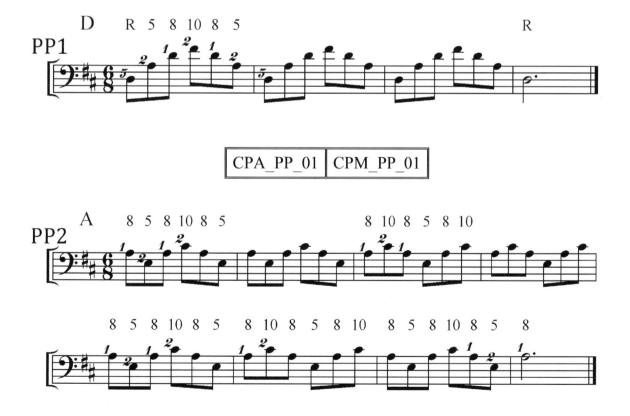

CPA_PP_02 | CPM_PP_02

CPA_PP_03 | CPM_PP_03

CPA_PP_04 | CPM_PP_04

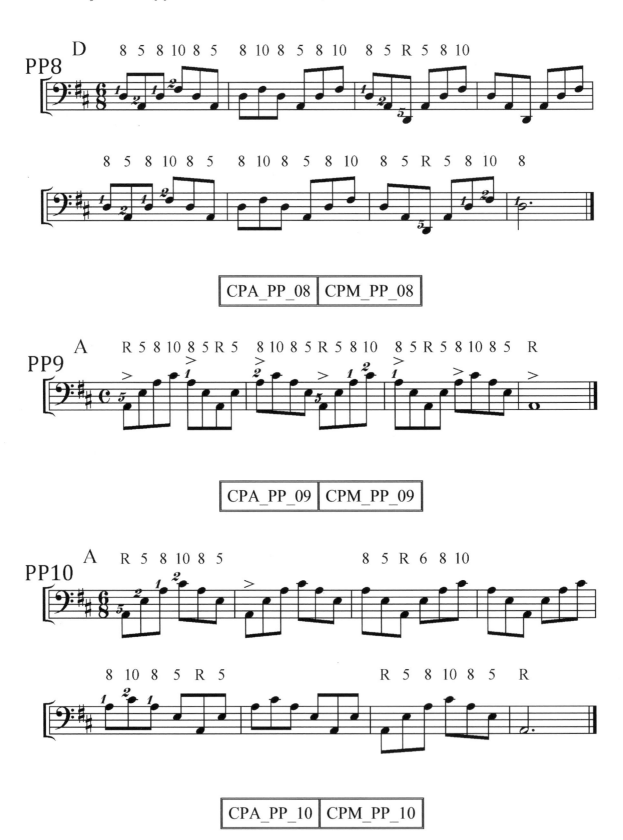

CPA_PP_11 | CPM_PP_11

CPA_PP_12 | CPM_PP_12

The Canon Diaries Supplement

The Canon Diaries are Musicarta's ongoing explorations of the Canon chord sequence, and demonstrate the kind of creative freedom you can expect to achieve if you study the Canon Project thoroughly and put what you have learnt into practice.

The Canon Diary 'entries' have all appeared on Mister Musicarta YouTube (MMYT), so there is video reference material to help guide your study. Here is the section TOC.

Canon Diaries 12-05-12 is a speedy run-through of the Canon chord sequence. The right hand uses triads, broken up. The bass uses only roots, but becomes highly syncopated, and explores the possibility of bouncing between notes of an octave. The modulation back from the B section gives rises to the following transposing exercise.

MMYT video 1: CD 12-05-12 Video One   Audio and MIDI folder: CD_1205 A & M

MMYT video 2: CD 12-05-12 Video Two

The CD 12-05-12 B strain modulates from F back into home key D major – a fall of a minor third. Using this modulation, you can rehearse the Canon chords in four keys

MMYT video: Transposing the Canon – Video   A & M folder: CD_TRA A & M

Canon Diaries 13-06-12 is a lyrical, open-textured repertoire piece with a mainly two-note left hand part, and plenty of opportunity to practice two-handed syncopation. It also features suspension-release and 'pedal point' harmonic constructions.

MMYT video: Canon Diaries 13-06-12 revisited   A & M folder: CD_1306 A & M

Musicarta's signature 'LH-over style' is an ideal plan for 'just playing chords'. Here, it is applied to the Canon chord sequence, with a collection of generic alternative endings, A2 and B strains.

MMYT video 1: Canon LHO Video 1   A & M folder: CD_LHO A & M

MMYT video 2: Canon LHO Video 2

MMYT video 3: Canon LHO Video 3

A full-on 'performance' Diary entry, showcasing accented (lowered) non-chord tones, and cycling through four keys. The drum track is included in the digital download.

MMYT video: Canon Diaries 01-09-13 video   A & M folder: CD_0109 A & M

Canon Diaries 12-05-12

The CD 12-05-12 Diary entry is a speedy run-through of the Canon chord sequence using just triads in the right hand and the root in the bass, and is intended as a quick chord work-out to sharpen up your chord sense.

The CD 12-05 version of the Canon chords has a contrasting 'B section' in the key of F, and so gives you the opportunity to practice transposing. This material gives rise to a follow-on Canon Transposing module. The entry also offers two alternative 'generic' endings, with full harmonic analysis, and the opportunity to practice syncopated left-hand bass lines.

There are two CD 12-05-12 Mister Musicarta YouTube videos. The first is the original, with a 'hands' performance and a second-half talk-through; the second video shows the performance on two MidiPiano keyboards, the actual performance on the lower keyboard and the 'skeleton chords' (the harmony chords before breaking up) on the upper one.

Here are the audio/video/MID references. Watch and listen as you read through the next few pages of notes before you start trying to play the version.

CD 12-05-12 Video One	
CD 12-05-12 Video Two	
CD_1205A_01	CD_1205M_01

Here are the bare chords of the first four-bar/eight-chord strain. (Watch out for the two bass clefs in the written music.)

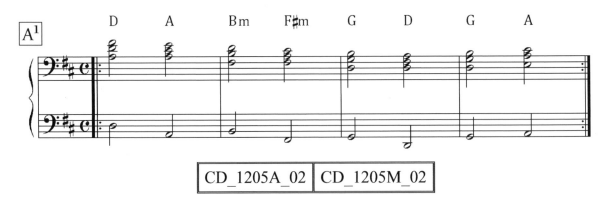

CD_1205A_02	CD_1205M_02

In performance, the right hand chord tones are broken up, with the second chord of each pair anticipated and the bass following the syncopation (see next MS example).

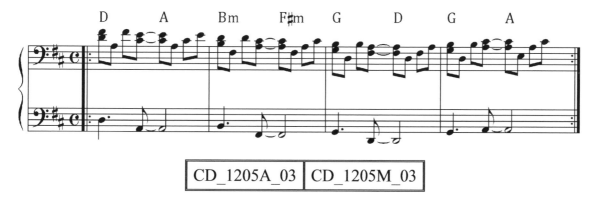

| CD_1205A_03 | CD_1205M_03 |

Your pop-styles musical ear should immediately be offering you a BMT (bottom, middle, top) analysis of the right hand pattern:

$$T\,B\,T\,T \ldots B\,M\,T \mid T\,B\,T\,T \ldots B\,M\,T$$

(The B/M/T chord tones are marked on the section keyboards, below.)

Because the second chord in each pair is pulled forward (anticipated), the third 'T' in the bar is the top note of the second chord in the pair. The first 'T' of each chord has the chord's 'M' with it. The first two bars of the MS (next page) have the full BMT analysis written in.

Check your understanding of this important bottom/middle/top (BMT) analysis. It was introduced in Module X of the Canon Project, and is an extremely fruitful way of thinking about chords.

AABA form

When used as a basis for songwriting, the lack of variety in the Canon chord sequence – with the same eight chords repeating endlessly – is an obvious shortcoming. One of the solutions suggested in the Musicarta Canon Project is adding a contrasting section to create a 32-bar AABA version, as you hear in CD 12-05-12 (and elsewhere). This development is discussed in Module Sixteen of the Canon Project work-book.

Here is the whole CD 12-05-12 AABA chord sequence.

1 (A¹ strain)

D	A	Bm	F♯m	G	D	G	A

9 (repeat A¹ strain)

D	A/C♯	Bm	F♯m/A	G	D/F♯	G	A

17 (B strain in F)   *(modulates back)*

F	C	Dm	Am	B♭	F	Gm	A

25 (A² strain)   *(novel ending)*

D	A	Bm	F♯m	B♭maj7	E♭maj7	D	D

Canon Diaries 12-05-12

Here are the keyboards for the first eight chords.

D

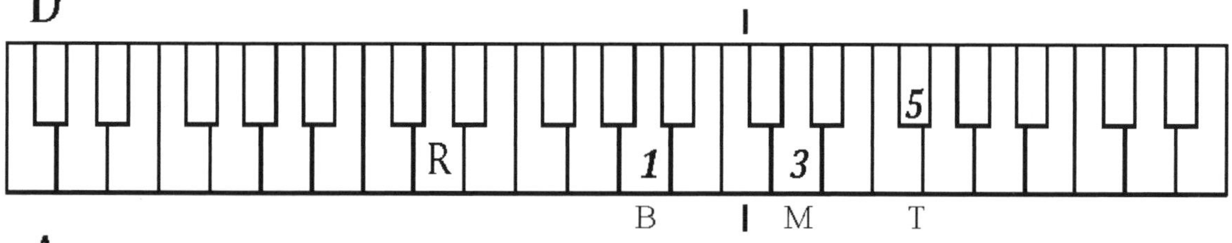

A

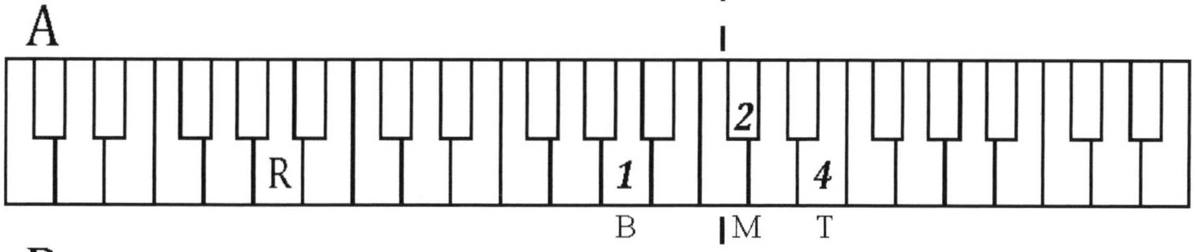

Bm

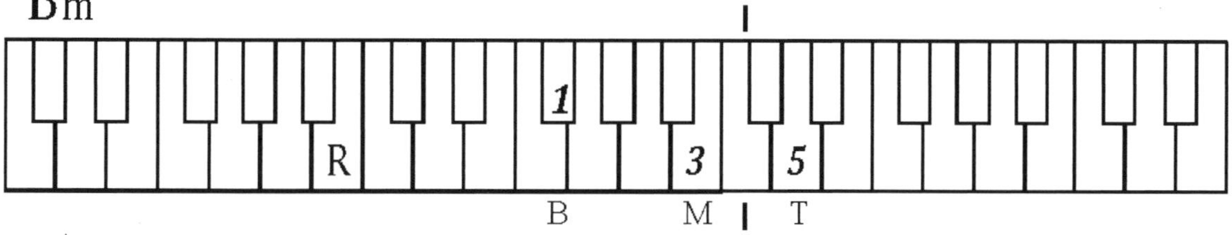

F♯m

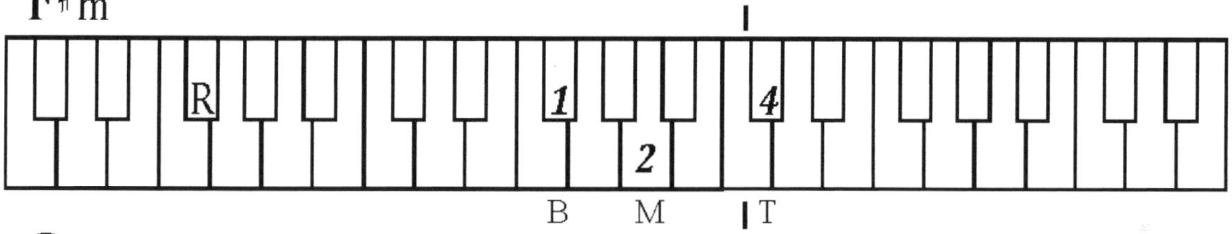

G

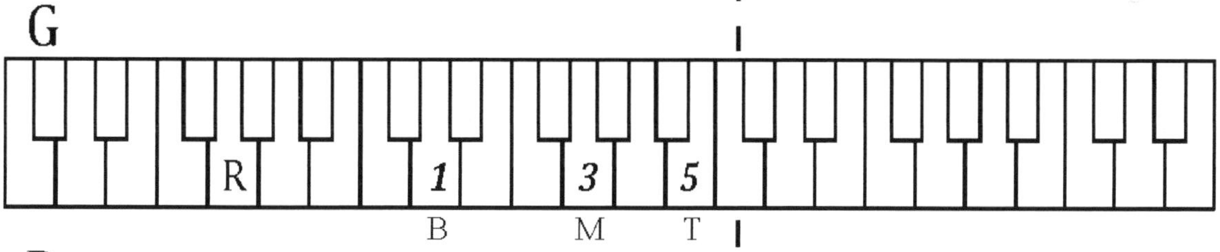

D

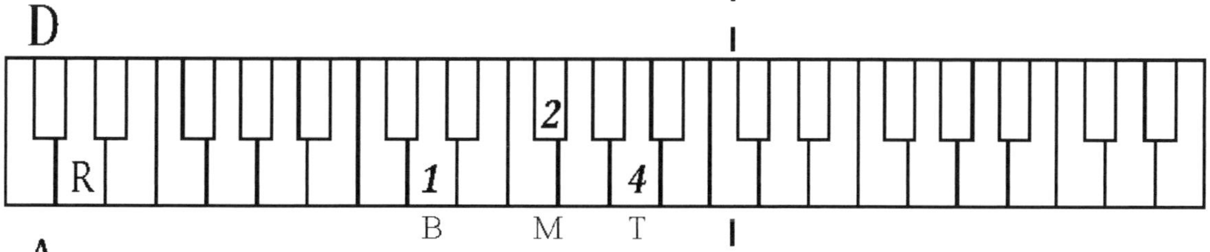

A

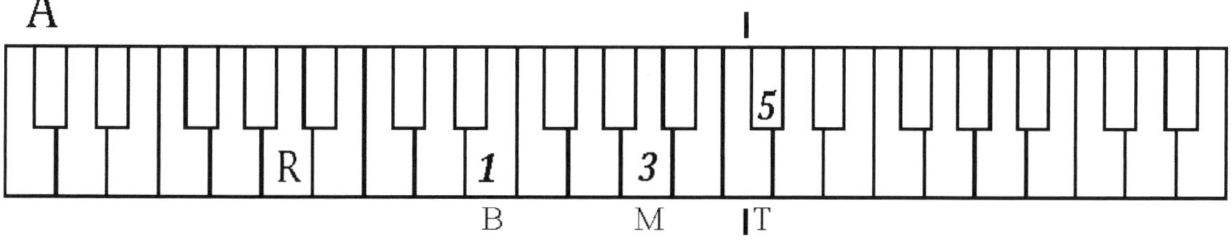

You can simply read the keyboards for the 'B strain' (next page) top to bottom.

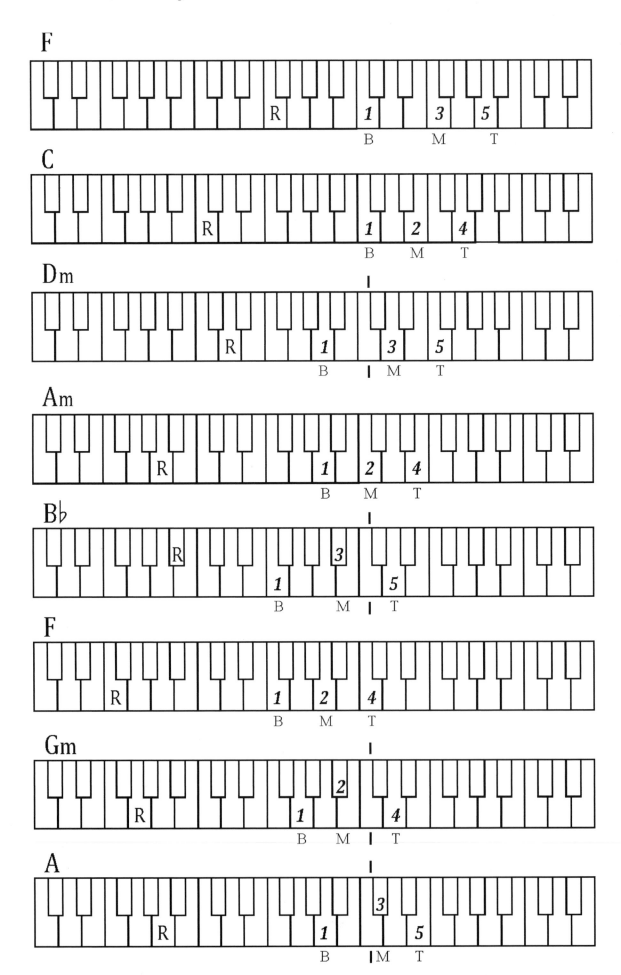

Here are the CD 12-05-12 skeleton chords, marked up AABA. These are the 'harmony chords' shown on the upper keyboard in the second module video,

The first strain is repeated, making a four-strain A^1 A^1 B A^2 form. The keyboards for the B section are on the previous page.

Various 'B sections' are offered in the Canon Project and Diary entries. As the talk-through in the second part of the first video explains, the B section here simply drops from the A chord at the end of the second A^1 strain into the key of F to play the I-V-vi-III-IV-I-IV-V Canon chord sequence, but modulating back into D in the last two chords, using Gm and A – ii and III of F and iv and V of D.

This modulating-back device is used in the Transposing module, next in the Supplement.

The bass line

You will decide yourself to what extent you want to develop the bass line (left hand). From the second strain of CD 12-05-12 on, it bounces between octaves and gets more caught up in the syncopation.

Written music of the actual notes is probably not helpful. In the long run, you will gain more by looking-and-listening to the MidiPiano Piano Roll view of the second CD 12-05-12 eight-chord strain than from any 'actual performance' music.

Here is a screen shot of the second strain, with the repeated audio/MIDI file references below. You can repeat the MIDI file on MidiPiano demo at your own chosen speed and play along until you get it. Some preparatory exercises follow.

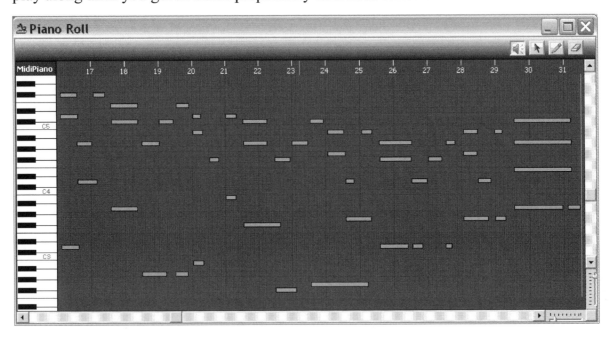

Here is a methodical bottom–top–top–bottom bass line exercise.

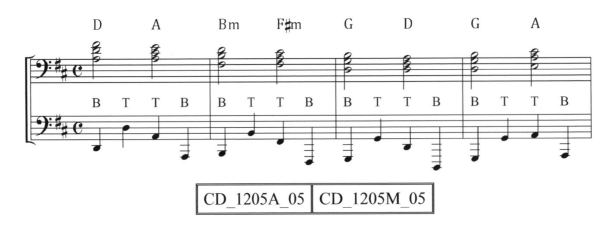

CD_1205A_05 | CD_1205M_05

Don't be bamboozled into actually reading those leger lines! The bass notes are all roots (the notes named in the chord symbols) – the chord symbol would tell you if it were another note (with, for example, a 'slash chord' symbol).

Now play the BTTB bass line under the broken-up right hand. (Your electronic keyboard might not go down as far as the lowest D. Just repeat the upper D if the octave-lower note isn't available.)

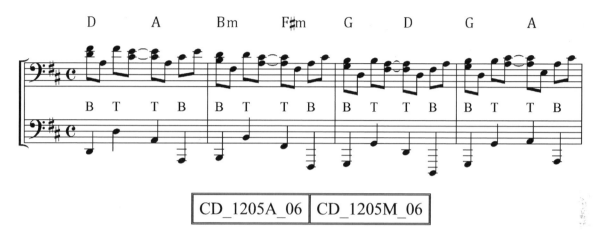

Here's a very syncopated bass line.

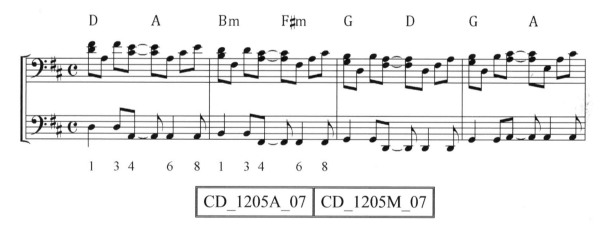

The numbers below the music are the quaver counts the left hand notes come on.

If you combine the two patterns (BTTB + syncopation), you get this.

Web_10 ✓✓

| CD_1205A_08 | CD_1205M_08 |

Here's a continuous-anticipation bass line (including pulling the next-chord roots forward over the bar-line):

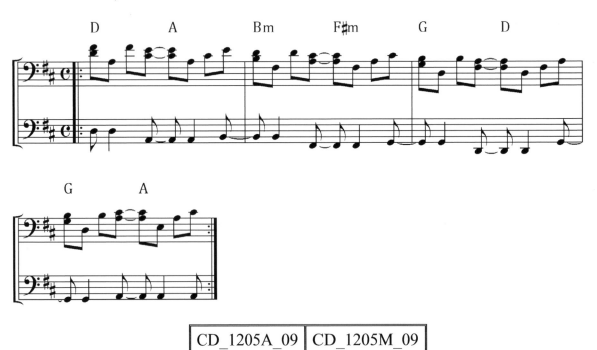

| CD_1205A_09 | CD_1205M_09 |

The bass guitar in Latin music sometimes anticipates every beat like this.

All of these effects, taken on their own and to extremes, become tiresome. These are exercises to practice so that you can anticipate beats and bounce between octaves (etc.) when it sounds good.

The endings

As pointed out in the talk-through (second part of the first video), the ending harmonises the final tonic (note D) in three successive chords – B flat major seven, E flat major seven and the final D chord (♭VImaj7–♭IImaj7–I) – a compelling harmony.

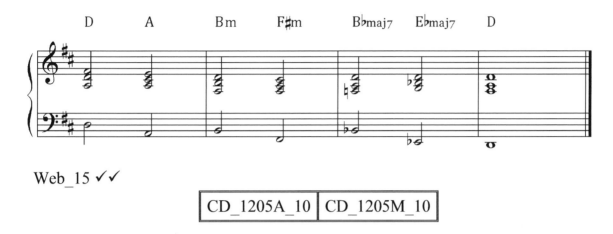

Web_15 ✓✓

| CD_1205A_10 | CD_1205M_10 |

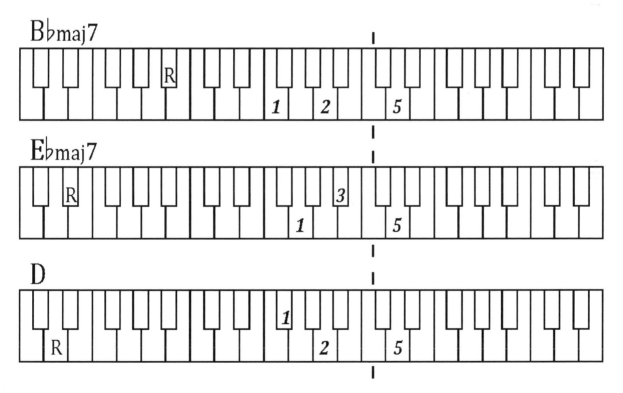

Played:

| CD_1205A_11 | CD_1205M_11 |

The harmonic logic is this. The final 'change' (chord change) is chord E flat to D, falling a semitone – which harmony will always do with very little prompting. The chord before that is B flat, which is a fifth above the E flat, making a perfect cadence (V–I, the most compelling harmonic movement).

An alternative ending which also harmonises three tonics (note D) and uses much the same dynamic, is this:

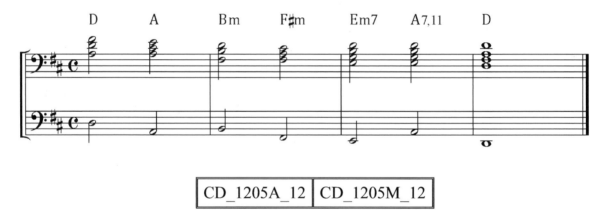

| CD_1205A_12 | CD_1205M_12 |

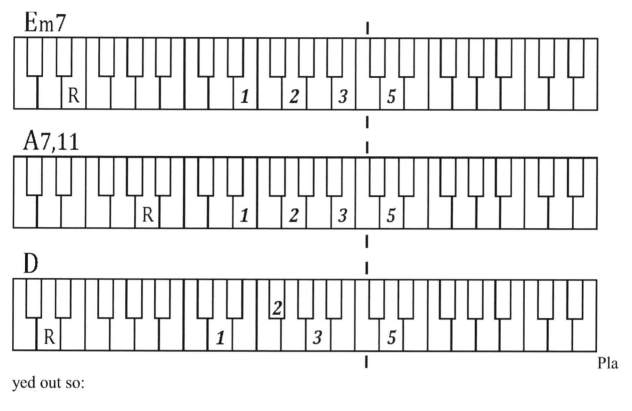

Em7

A7,11

D

Pla

yed out so:

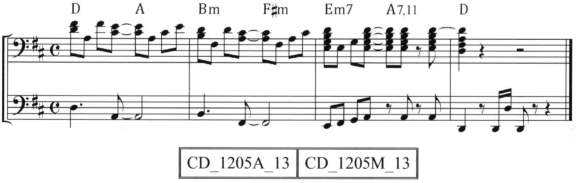

| CD_1205A_13 | CD_1205M_13 |

This is a ii–V–I, 'circle of fifths' construction. The final chord change is V7–I (A7–D), dominant to tonic – the 'perfect cadence'. The chord before that is ii7 (Em7), which is the (minor) dominant of the A chord – the 'secondary dominant'. This back-up-the-line 'dominant of the dominant' sequence is known as the circle of fifths.

This 12-05-12 Canon Diary entry offers a perfect opportunity to practice simply 'playing chords'. The amount of syncopation you achieve is immaterial – unless that happens to be the focus of your practicing.

CD 12-05-12 also offers an opportunity to study modulation and transposing, as explored in the next section of the Supplement.

Transposing the Canon chord sequence

Transposing is, in a sense, THE musical skill. Being able to play a piece of music or a chord sequence in another key 'just like that' testifies to real understanding of harmony, which in turn becomes a major creative asset.

Simple repetition is a tried and tested way of acquiring this skill. With repetition, you start to see the internal 'architecture' of the chord progression. The B strain of the 12-05-12 Canon Diary (previous section) offers a good way of practicing this.

Here are the audio/video/MIDI file references for this module.

Transposing the Canon – Video	
CD_TRA_01	CD_TRM_01

The CD 12-05-12 B strain is in F, and comprises these chords:

The first six chords are the Canon chord sequence chords in F. Expressed in Roman numerals (in the key of F), the chords are:

F	C	Dm	Am	B♭	F	G	A
I	V	vi	iii	IV	I	ii	III

The final III chord is the dominant (V) chord that returns us to the home key of D (next strain). The last three chords of the F strain (I-ii-III – F, Gm, A) where A (III) is V of D therefore lowers the key by (modulates down by) a minor third (F major down to D).

There are four minor thirds intervals to an octave, so if we play this modulating sequence, starting in D, we will drop successive minor thirds through B, A flat and F majors before returning to D.

This exercise will give the invaluable experience of playing most of the Canon chord sequence in four different keys.

The chords for this exercise are on the next page. The first chord in each line of music is the tonic – you are playing in the key of that chord, and that is the key signature you see.

The last phrase of the audio/video material (back in D) ends with the ♭VImaj7–♭IImaj7–I chords from CD 12-05-12.　　　Web_6

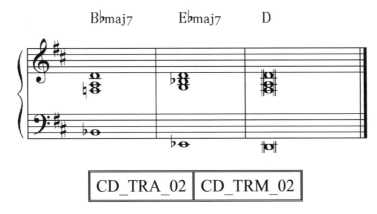

| CD_TRA_02 | CD_TRM_02 |

You could instead – when you get back into D – play the final A^2 strain of the original CD 12-05-12, or use the alternative Em7–A7,11 ending. Try both, for comparison.

'Modulating'

Changing key in the course of a piece is called modulating.

Pop songs often modulate – both for dramatic, musical effect and to sweeten repetition for the listener. Sometimes only a section is in the new key and the song modulates back, and sometimes the song or piece ends in the new key.

In music theory, modulation is traditionally notated using the Roman numeral system, like this (the first modulation in this series, D to B):

	D	A	Bm	F♯m	G	D	Em	F♯	
Key of D:	I	V	vi	iii	IV	I	ii	III	
Key of B:							iv	V	I	V	vi
							Em	F♯	B	F♯	G♯m

The overlap shows the modulating chords (E minor and F♯ major) written in both keys – as ii and III in D, and as iv and V in new key B major. The overlapping chords are also called 'common chords' or 'pivot chords'.

It is quite possible that you will feel quite 'lost' during this exercise – it is certainly a step up in complexity. 'Slogging on through' is not regular Musicarta advice, but, in this case, it is! Use the Key-specific Keyboards PDF (in your download) to help you start seeing the keyboard in complicated keys like B and A flat major.

.

Canon Diaries 13-06-12

Canon Diaries 13-06-12 is a lyrical, open-textured repertoire piece with a mainly two-note left hand part, and plenty of opportunity to practice two-handed syncopation. It also features suspension-release as a composing-at-the-keyboard technique, and highlights the 'pedal point' harmonic construction.

CD 13-06-12 is another 'revisited' entry, so there are two Mister Musicarta YouTube videos, the original one of which is now archived. The notes here refer to the revised version.

CD 13-06-12 (archive) video	
CD_1306A_01	CD_1306M_01
Canon Diaries 13-06-12 revisited	

Getting the syncopated rhythms

Whether you are working from the written music (MS) or trying to work a piece like this out by ear, your first move should be to try to see/hear the simple elements underneath the fancy 'realization' (performance).

In CD 13-06, that means this 'essentials-only' material (first phrase). CD13-06_01

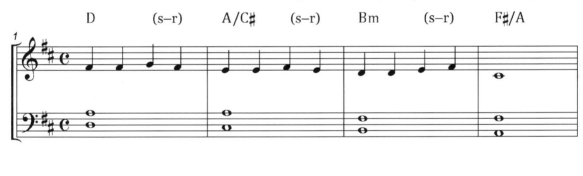

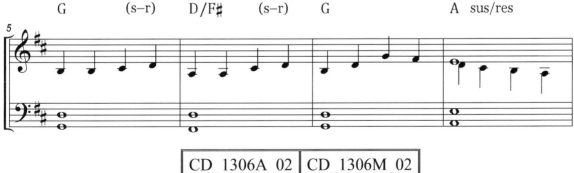

CD_1306A_02	CD_1306M_02

Right hand syncopation

You would probably try to master the syncopation of the right hand only, first. Comparing the 'essentials-only' MS with the performance MS, you see that beats three and four in the right hand are anticipated, that is, dragged forward a quaver off the beat. The last note in the first line is even dragged forward across the bar line.

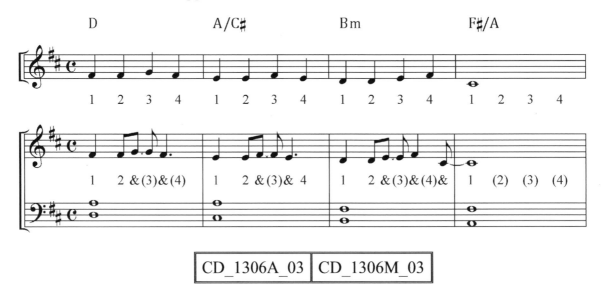

| CD_1306A_03 | CD_1306M_03 |

The audio/MIDI files demo just the first four bars, repeated.

Practice tip: Load the MIDI in MidiPiano, select Repeat, adjust Speed and play along until effortless. Then add next four bars for the whole first phrase.

Mastering the syncopation one hand at a time is the efficient way to work! Be aware of the temptation to skip these build-up steps – they build a solid foundation.

Left hand syncopation

Next, look at the left hand (just look!). The counting tracks only the left hand notes. Counts in brackets, e.g. (2), indicate where a note **isn't** played. Eliminating the tied notes, we see there are only left hand notes played on counts 1 &, & 4 &.

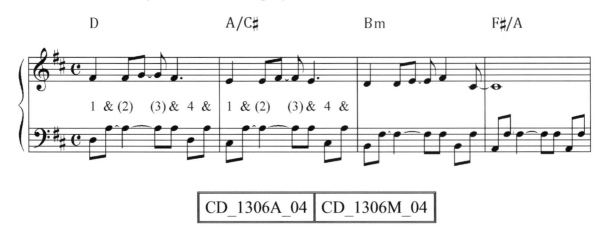

| CD_1306A_04 | CD_1306M_04 |

Hopefully you spotted that this rhythm is used for virtually the whole of the piece. It's much more efficient to learn a pattern – a template – and pour the notes into it, than to learn a whole string of notes one by one.

Here are some syncopation practice techniques.

- Listen to the practice speed audio and count the left hand out aloud.

- Practise the left hand movement on your desktop using fingers 5 and 1.

- Loop the audio in Audacity to give yourself time to ease into the rhythm.

- Try playing the left hand under right hand crotchet chords.

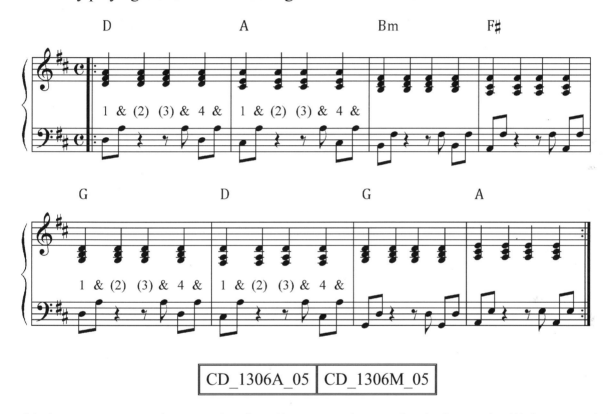

| CD_1306A_05 | CD_1306M_05 |

This is great syncopation practice for all your modern-style playing and will free your left hand to play off the beat in many circumstances.

The 'sticky' left hand

The music above leaves out all the tied CD 13-06 left hand notes. In practice, the CD 13-06 left hand is played as 'sticky' as possible, that is, both notes are held for as much of the time as possible and only come up to be played again.

Here's a MidiPiano picture of the 'sticky' style. (The proper musical expression is *tenuto*, Italian for 'held'.)

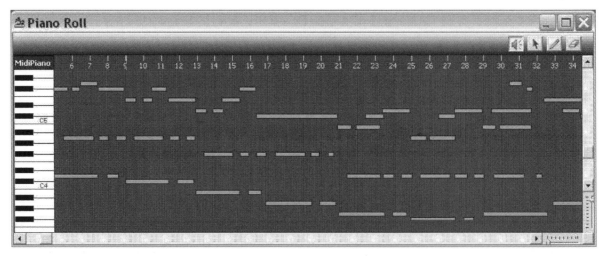

Music accurately showing these note-lengths is even more difficult to read. (See below. In general, syncopated popular-styles music is even more difficult to read than classical music. That's why Musicarta offers so many alternative ways to learn.)

| CD_1306A_06 | CD_1306M_06 |

The audio referred is the first phrase of the actual performance. Practise your listening skills and see if you can hear how the left hand notes stay down until they're needed again, and only then raised and played again.

This 'sticky' left hand style is harder to achieve than the simple see-saw, one up-one down rocking style. Keep working at it. – one day you 'just can'!

TLR analysis: two-handed syncopation

The next step in to work out 'what comes with what'. Musicarta calls this TLR (together, left, right) analysis, and it's a crucial step in mastering syncopated two-handed playing.

Here is the first section with the TLR analysis sketched in. The counting now tracks the notes in both hands.

Practice tip: Rehearse these patterns away from the keyboard first, on an imaginary desktop keyboard, so you don't have to worry about getting the right notes to start with.

| CD_1306A_07 | CD_1306M_07 |

You see immediately that in the 'typical' bars, only count 3 **doesn't** have a note on it. Also, despite what the music looks like (and what you think you hear), there aren't many 'T' (together) 'events'.

Abandon the rhythm entirely as you try to get your performance going. You're only interested in getting the right together/left/right 'events' in the right order (with the right notes). The rhythm can wait until your muscles are happy with the TLR sequence.

Moving to the piano keyboard, here are the first four bars (first line of music above) played TLR, without rhythm.

| CD_1306A_08 | CD_1306M_08 |

When you can play the typical TLR sequence, gradually speed up. Work on just the first two bars. If you then make the fourth note in the bar (the second 'R') longer, it will spread over into the 'nothing-happens' count 3, and you will have the rhythm too.

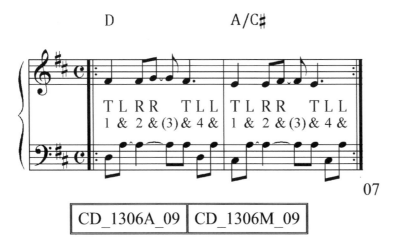

| CD_1306A_09 | CD_1306M_09 |

Practice tip: Load the MIDI file into MidiPiano, set the 'Repeat' function, use 'Speed' to slow it down to a comfortable speed and play along. Listen critically to tighten up your performance. If at all possible, tap your foot to the beat as well.

Perform this 'dissect and build up' method throughout. Pencil in the counts and the TLR analysis on your hard copy. It doesn't have to be neat or even right – making a focussed technical effort is what gets you there!

The harmony

Chord sequence

Here is the revised CD 13-06-12 chord sequence. The overall form is AABA.

1 (A¹ strain)

| D | A/C♯ | Bm | F♯m/A | G | D/F♯ | G | A |

9 (repeat A¹ strain)

| D | A/C♯ | Bm | F♯m/A | G | D/F♯ | G | A |

17 (B strain)

| F♯/A♯ | Bm | A/C♯ | D | G | G | Em7 | Em7 |

25 (pedal point extension)

| G/A: | G/A: | G/A: | A7 sus- |
| F♯m/A | F♯m/A | F♯m/A | res |

29 (A² phrase)

| D | A/C♯ | G/B | F♯m/A | G | D/F♯:Bm | G:F♯m/A | A7 |

37 (extended ending)

| D :G/D | G/D:A/D | D | D |

The extension of the Canon chord sequence to something approaching song length – by inserting a contrasting 'B section' – is discussed in Module 16 of the Canon Project.

Being aware of overall structure in this way is an essential part of songwriting and composing. The original Canon Diaries 13-06-12 entry was $A^1 A^1 B A^1 A^2$ form. You might still prefer that. Put the extra A^1 back in, if you like.

Chord symbols

Note these two points.

- Slash chords. A chord symbol such as A/C♯ indicates that a note other than the root (name-note) of the chord is being played in the bass (by the left hand). The example given (A/C♯) indicates an A chord with a C♯ in the bass.

- Bars with two chord symbols and a colon in the middle (e.g. D :G/D) indicate a bar that is split between two chords. The example given indicates a bar split between a D chord and a G chord with D in the bass.

Special feature: Suspension-release

Suspensions are showcased in CD 13-06 as a technique four your own composing-at-the-keyboard. You can experiment with pulling any chord tone up (or pushing it down) a scale step.

- Where suspensions occur on the main (first) beat they are indicated sus/res.

- Where they occur on any other beat they are indicated (s–r) (skeleton music only).

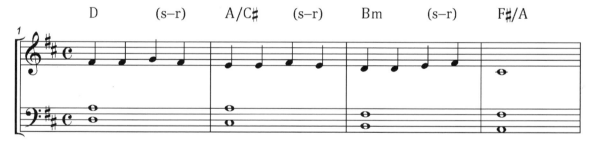

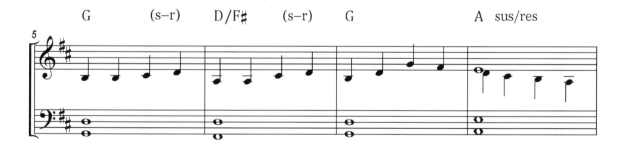

Suspensions here means any 'accented non-chord tones', including notes **below** the chord tone they resolve to ('accented lower auxiliaries'). Identify examples in the music above: note E in B minor chord bar 3, the accented C♯ in bar 5, and the C♯ in bar 6.

(discussion continues after MS)

Canon Diaries 13-06-12

(continued)

Suspensions are a great way to get more songwriting 'mileage' out of chords, and focussed study will also develop your playing-by-ear. Find more examples of suspensions via the Suspensions tab on the Musicarta site navbar and on the Mister Musicarta YouTube Suspensions playlist.

Special feature: Pedal points

A pedal point is a section of music with a single bass note, held or repeated regardless of changing chords above it. Example, bars 25-28:   graphic 08

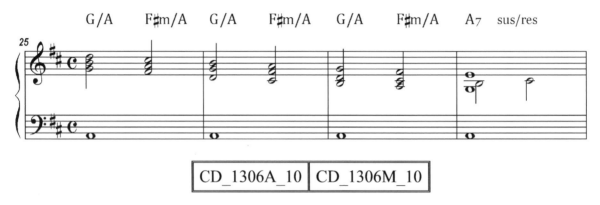

Notice that there are only two chords in the upper part (right hand) – G and F#m. They 'keep coming' because the music cycles down through root position, second and first inversions of the alternating chords.

Learn the skeleton chords first. In performance, they are broken up T B M T (top, bottom, middle, top – with an additional 'M' thrown in!).

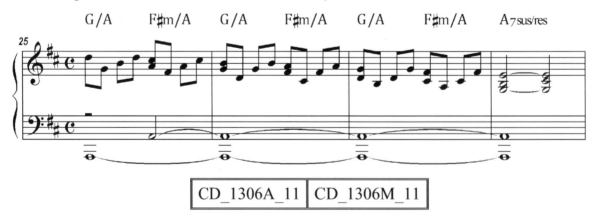

This pedal point material keeps the tension up because the G chord over A is essentially an A7sus chord, only resolving to A7 the very last chord.

There is more pedal point material at bars 35 to 38, first over bass A, then finally over tonic D. Note that 'slash chord' chord symbols used to notate the pedal point material.

Canon chords in LH-over texture

To play chords at the keyboard – to 'just sit down and play' – you need to know your chord tones and have a rhythmic texture, a plan for playing them. This Canon Diary entry showcases the realisation (playing out) of a chord sequence using the Musicarta left hand over texture – left hand bass and LH-over notes with regular right hand broken chord patterns.

Musicarta has released two extended teach-yourself piano solos which employ the LH-over texture – Chords for Carl and Mariaan. You can find these and other samples in the Mister Musicarta YouTube 'LH-over' playlist.

This learning module shows the chord tones on keyboards as well as giving the music. Even if you are a proficient reader, the keyboards offer an opportunity to develop your 'seeing the music in the keyboard' skills.

Here are the audio/video/MIDI references for the first Canon LH-over version we will be studying.

Canon LHO Video 1	
CD_LHA_01	CD_LHM_01

Read through the first three sections of the following material (as far as 'RH broken chord patterns') as you look-and-listen to the first video, and before you start playing.

The chord sequence

Here is the chord sequence of the music you have just heard.

1
| D | A/C♯ | Bm | F♯m/A | G | D/F♯ | G | A |

9
| D | A/C♯ | Bm | F♯m/A | G | D/F♯ | G | A |

17
| F♯/A♯ | Bm | A/C♯ | D | G6 | G6 | A7sus | A7 |

25
| D | A/C♯ | Bm | F♯m/A | G | D/F♯ | G | A |

33
| D | D/A | D | D |

Here is the 'skeleton' music – just the basic right hand chords and bass notes, before any keyboard texture is applied (excludes LH-over notes).

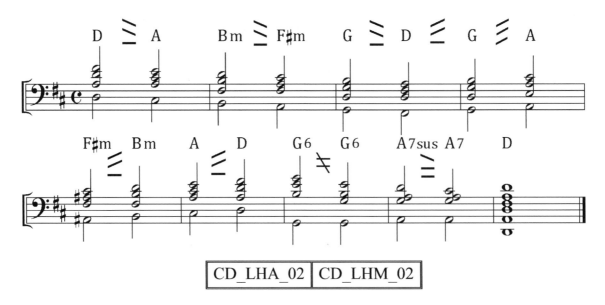

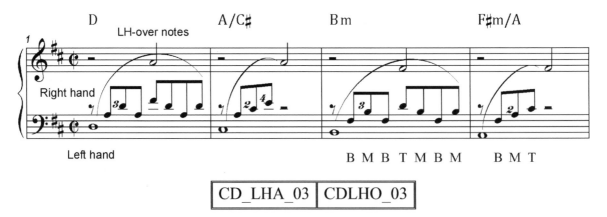

To become a creative, 'in charge' keyboard musician, it is essential that you cultivate a habit of figuring out (and thoroughly mastering!) the basic elements beneath the music you hear. You need to 'own' this material in order to compose and improvise successfully.

Note the voice movement diagram (VMD) between the right hand chords. These help you keep track of how the chord tones change to form the next chord. Voice movement diagrams are explained in the Canon Project home study work-book.

Understanding the written music (MS)

Here is a sample of the Canon LH-over MS:

(The audio/MIDI reference files repeat at practice speed.)

Notice how the music for the left and right hands is written on the staves.

- The left hand bass notes are the lowest notes.

- The right hand broken-chord notes are written on the bass clef (lower) stave, but stems-up.

- The treble (upper) clef is reserved for the left-hand-over notes.

The MS for the whole performance is given further on in the module. Canon LH-over page 1, 2.

The keyboards

All the notes in this piece can be indicated on keyboard diagrams (next two pages). The new Canon chords in LH-over texture Mister Musicarta YouTube videos show the relevant individual keyboard diagrams (coloured) above the MidiPiano performance.

Here are the first four chords in the chord sequence shown on keyboards. The full set of keyboards for the video performance is given further on in the module.

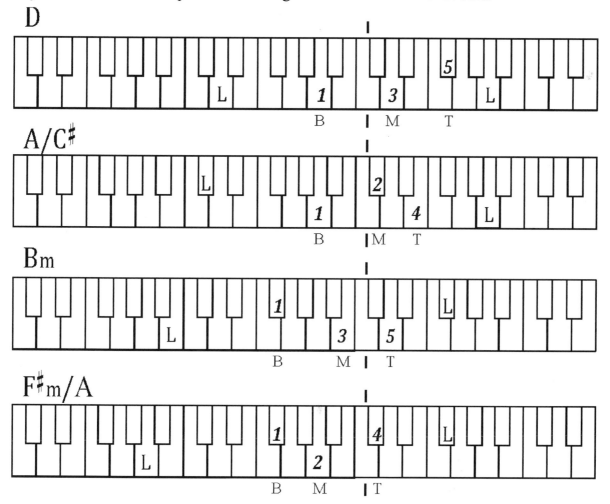

To keep your printing costs to a minimum, the Canon Project work-book is in black and white. To get the greatest benefit, you would colour in the keyboards using fluorescent markers matching the green = left, orange = right colour scheme of the Mister Musicarta YouTube channel videos. This in itself forms part of the learning process.

This is the music these keyboards represent (as before).

| CD_LHA_03 | CDLHO_03 |

Now we go on to see how you can use both the music and the keyboards to learn to play the music.

The RH broken chord patterns

This is the written music (MS) for the audio file above. Study it without playing for now.

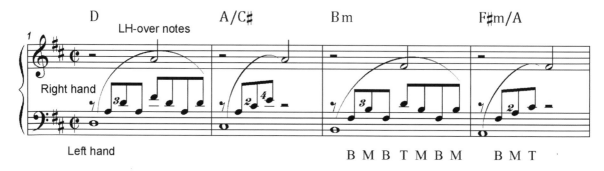

The right hand covers a triad (three-note chord) indicated by the green finger-numbered keys on the keyboards. For our analysis of the right hand pattern, we designate these B = bottom, M = middle, T = top.

The usual order of the right hand chord tones (two-bar pattern) is:

B M B T M B M | B M T

This is indicated under bars 3 and 4 in the music. Listen to the Module performance and try to hear the pattern.

This pattern stays exactly the same until indicated otherwise. Examples:

- In bar 10 (and the even-numbered bars which follow): B M B T (instead of just B M T)

- Bars 17 to 20 (new two-bar pattern):

B M B T B M T | B M T

- Bars 21 to 23, all: B M B T M B M

Then back to the original pattern until the repeated B M B T M B M of the ending.

Placing the left hand notes

Still studying away from the keyboards, notice the placement of the left hand notes. The typical two-bar pattern is:

```
              L                                    L
      B  M  B  T  M  B  M  |      B  M  T
  L                            L
```

In the second eight-bar phrase (bars 9 to 16) the second of each pair of bars is different, and the pattern is:

```
              L                                    L
      B  M  B  T  M  B  M  |      B  M  B  T
  L                            L
```

In bars 17 to 20 the first bar is different, and the pattern is:

```
              L                                    L
      B  M  B  T  B  M  T  |      B  M  T
  L                            L
```

These are the only patterns that occur.

Playing the music from the keyboard diagrams

The first phrase is two pairs of bars on this pattern:

```
              L                                    L
      B  M  B  T  M  B  M  |      B  M  T
  L                            L
```

Using the keyboards for the first four chords (next page), go ahead and play the first phrase. (This audio file presents the four bars repeated, at practice speed.)

| CD_LHA_03 | CD_LHM_03 |

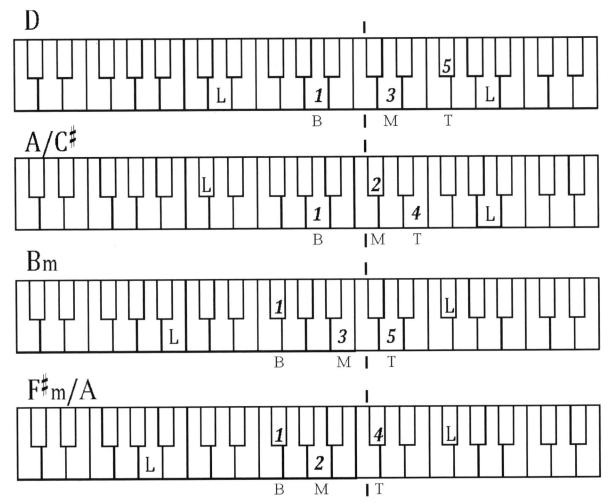

To boost your practice efficiency, the rest of this performance is offered in repeating practice-speed segments according to this table.

Bars 5 to 8: CD_LHA/M_04	Bars 9 to12: CD_LHA/M_05
Bars 13 to16: CD_LHA/M_06	Bars 17 to 20: CD_LHA/M_07
Bars 21 to 24: CD_LHA/M_08	Bars 33 to 36: CD_LHA/M_09

Remember, you can loop audio files in Audacity (and elsewhere), and MidiPiano can repeat segments and slow them down even more.

Playing the whole performance

The full set of keyboards is on the next two pages. The written music is after that. The BMT coding in the written music tells you which of the keyboard patterns to use. Carry on using the same pattern until you get 'new instructions'.

Using the two in combination as suits your abilities, play the whole performance.

CD_LHA_01	CD_LHM_01

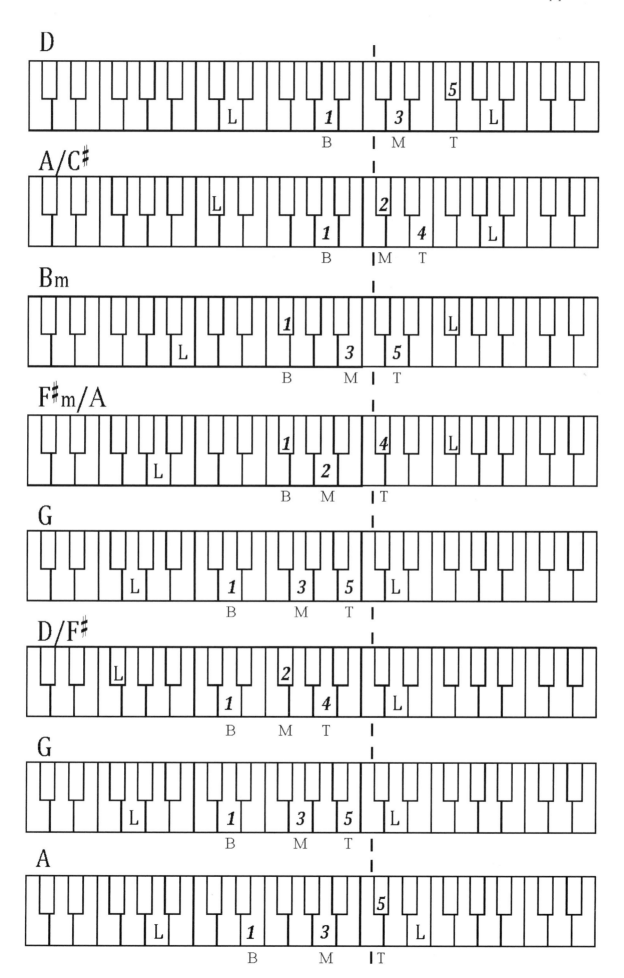

Canon chords in LH-over texture

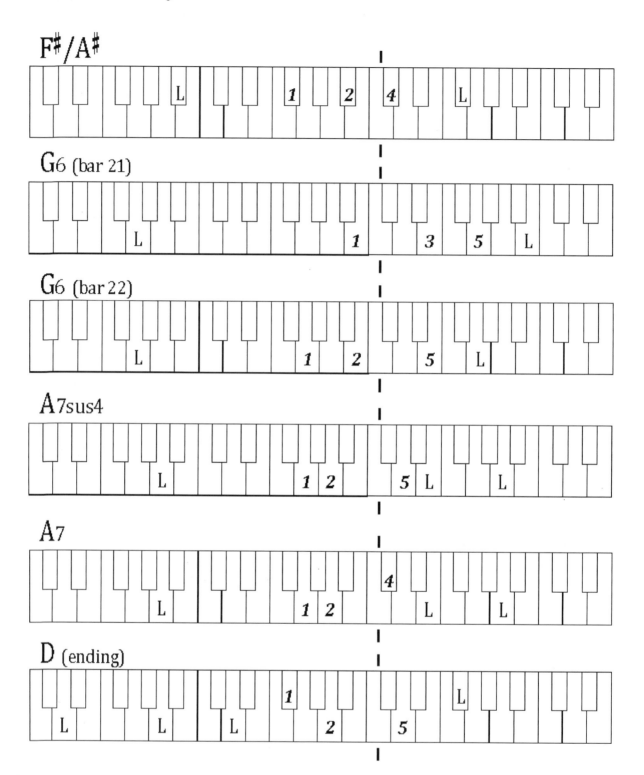

An alternative ending

Listen to this alternative ending.

CD_LHA_10	CD_LHM_10

Here is the music for the new ending. The keyboards are on the next page.

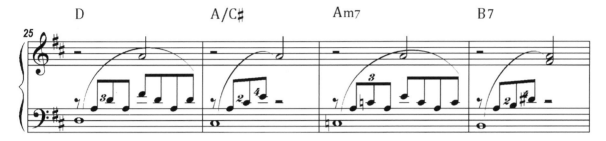

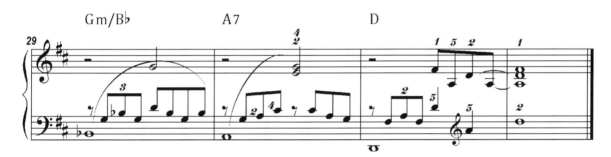

Write in the BMT analysis under the music and try to reproduce the performance from the music and keyboards combined. The final D chord is split between left and right hand keyboards.

The second Canon LH-over video shows a performance with this new ending. Here are the audio/video/MIDI file references, followed by the performance chord sequence.

Canon LHO Video 2	
CD_LHA_11	CD_LHM_11

1

D	A/C♯	Bm	F♯m/A	G	D/F♯	G	A

9

D	A/C♯	Bm	F♯m/A	G	D/F♯	G	A

17

F♯/A♯	Bm	A/C♯	D	G6	G6	A7sus	A7

25

D	A/C♯	Am/C	B7	Gm/B♭	A7	D	D

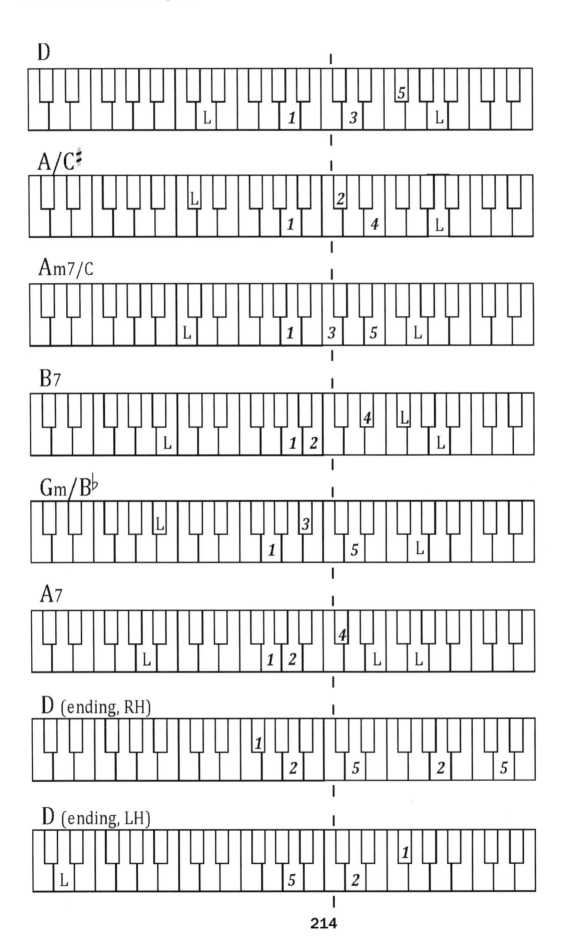

An alternative 'middle eight'

The 'B' strain in AABA form is sometimes known as 'the middle eight', even though it doesn't occur exactly in the middle. Refer to the discussion of AABA form in Module Sixteen of the Canon Project work-book.

Here is the music for the alternative 'middle eight'. The keyboards are on the next page.

| CD_LHA_12 | CD_LHM_12 |

This is the B section of Canon Diaries 12-05-12 with mediant substitution in every other bar (the even-numbered bars). Mediant substitution is discussed in Module Sixteen of the Canon Project work-book.

There is a video of this version on MMYT. It has the alternative ending from the previous version. As before, you could play an AABAA version, if you think that sounds better.

Canon LHO Video 3	
CD_LHA_13	CD_LHM_13

Make up your own chord sequence

Using the combined keyboard diagrams in this Pyramids Diaries section, you can easily put together new chord sequences in D. Play the LH-over texture in D, and try moving to any near-by right hand chords – the bass can jump around. If something doesn't sound quite right, try changing notes one at a time. A page of blank keyboard diagrams is provided at the end of the work-book for you to record the chord sequences you discover.

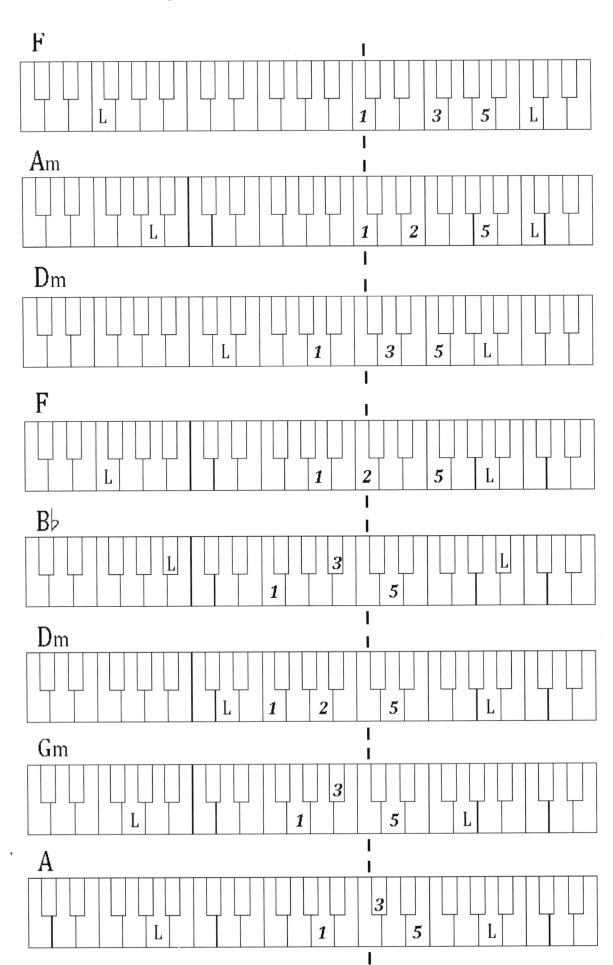

Canon Diaries 01-09-13

Canon Diaries 01-09-13 is a no-holds-barred suspensions-and-modulation showcase to round off the Canon Diaries Supplement of the revised, re-issued Musicarta Canon Project.

Detailed learning notes are not given, but if you apply all the tips and techniques detailed in the previous Diary entry learning notes, you are bound to get something sweet into your repertoire!

Here are the links and file references.

Canon Diaries 01-09-13 video	
CD_0109A_01	CD_0109M_01

Canon Diaries 01-09-13 chord sequence

Here is the CD 01-09-13 chord sequence. Notice that we are starting in the key of F.

'A^1' strain – regular Canon chord sequence in F

F	C	Dm	Am	B♭	F	B♭	C

Repeat 'A' strain

F	C	Dm	Am	B♭	F	B♭	C

New 'B' strain – chord sequence in A♭ (= ♭III)

A♭	E♭	Fm	Cm	D♭	A♭	B♭m7	C

'A^2' – chord sequence back in F

F	C	Dm	Am	B♭	F	B♭	C

Extended ending

F	B♭/F	F	F

Surprise 'in G' version – 'B' strain chord sequence, ending on chord B

G	D	Em	Bm	C	G	Am	B

… and modulating ('III=V') into E for final 'A' strain

E	B	C♯m	G♯m	A	C♯m	F♯m:E/G♯	A :B

Extended ending

E	A/E	E	A/E	E	A/E	E	E

Features

Accented non-chord tones

More than half the melody notes in CD 01-09-13 are non-chord tones (mainly lowered). Because there are so many of them, the suspensions are not marked in the chord symbols.

The Mister Musicarta YouTube Canon Diaries 01-09-13 video shows the right hand 'skeleton chords', before any syncopation is applied. Note the colour coding: non-moving chord tones are coded green, and the orange tone is the melody note. (Usually, green is the bass/left hand part.)

The melody note is usually at the top of the chord, but as the melody gets lower, it is more likely to be the middle or even the bottom note of the chord. (Triads start getting a little 'muddy' below middle C.)

You will find the skeleton chords MIDI file in your download. Always learn the basics first! Once you have that, take a close looks at the MIDI performance in MidiPiano.

> CD_0109M_02

Syncopation

There is an elaborate bouncing bass (bounces between lower and upper notes of an octave), but it is unlikely that you would play exactly the composer's bass part, which is pretty spontaneous (CD 01-09-13 is a transcribed performance) and is dictated by the syncopation of the right hand part, anyway – which you are also unlikely to play exactly 'as written'.

You could make a viable attempt at cribbing this piece from just the video. Copy the right hand skeleton chord-and-moving note part and supply an octave root (or slash chord bass). Then, just let it get funky!

Note that the full MS, audio and MIDI files ship with the new edition (end 9/13) Canon Project. The MS also gives the right hand skeleton music. It cannot be emphasised strongly enough that becoming wholly familiar with the underlying musical material, before trying to build up two-handed syncopation, is essential

Using any basic MIDI editor (there are plenty available free on the Internet – Anvil is quite user-friendly), you can chop the MIDI file into practice segments which you can repeat and slow down on MidiPiano.

Getting just one syncopated segment down per session in this way, however simplified it might be, should be celebrated as an acceptable achievement. "It all adds up!" One pattern per week – equals a whole style of playing in just a year!

(To minimise page turns, your blank keyboards appear next.
The discussion of CD 01-09-13 continues after MS.)

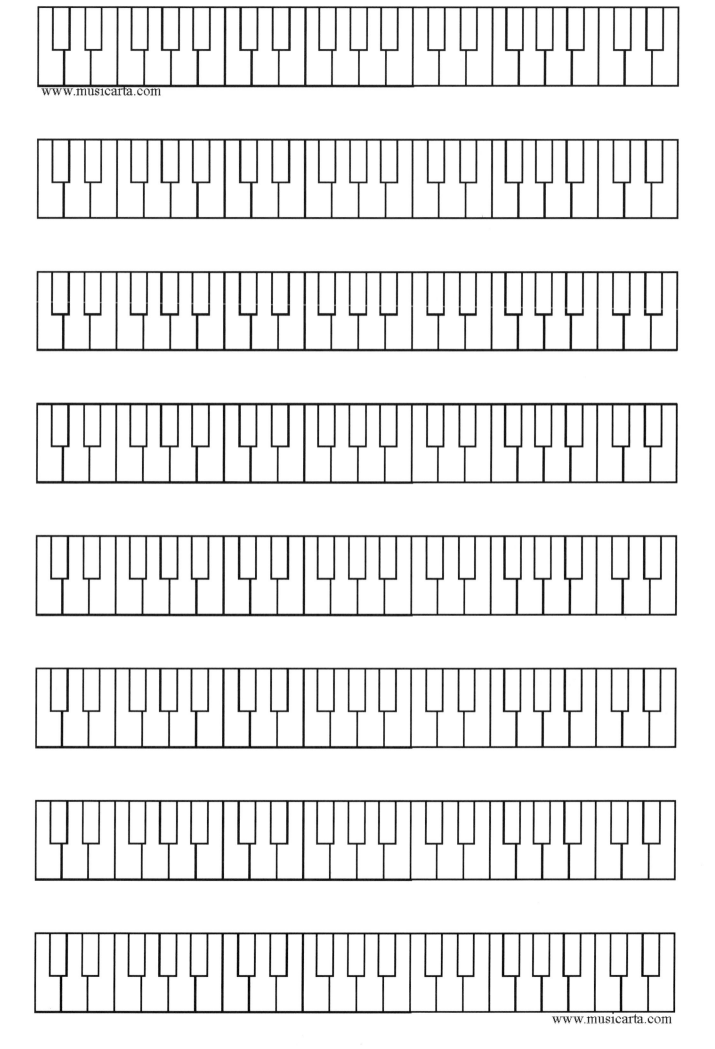

www.musicarta.com

Canon Diaries 01-09-13

Modulation and transposing

Canon Diaries 01-09-13 presents the basic Canon chord sequence in no less than four keys: F, A♭, G and E (first, third, sixth and seventh lines of the chord sequence). The surprise re-start in G (line six) is very noticeable, but hardly anyone will spot the final modulation into E.

The modulations make for exciting listening. You would not play a Canon-based chord sequence of this length without modulating 'to sweeten the pill'. It also gives you, the player, invaluable experience, and builds real 'in-any-key' understanding of harmony.

Postscript

The Musicarta Canon Project offers an excellent basis for learning how to play, and play with, chords at the keyboard. Continuing 'Canon Diary' entries on Mister Musicarta YouTube – and their associated web pages – present the creative musician with a stimulus to keep exploring the potential of this rich harmonic mother-lode.

With a little preliminary study – and with the chord sequence thoroughly memorised! – all the free-to-air Musicarta Canon material on the home website and at Mister Musicarta YouTube can easily be used to practice playing by ear.

Here is a collection of web URLS for relevant Musicarta Canon Project internet material. Paste them into your browser address bar, click through, and bookmark the pages in a dedicated section in your bookmarks pane, to inspire and support your studying.

Musicarta – the home site: http://www.musicarta.com/index.html, and the Canon Project home page: http://www.musicarta.com/Pachelbel_Canon_in_D_major.html

> Get the Musicarta site RSS feed for instant updates: www.musicarta.com/piano-lessons-online.xml, or bookmark the site blog http://www.musicarta.com/piano-lessons-online-blog.html and check in from time to time.

Mister Musicarta YouTube (MMYT): http://www.youtube.com/user/MisterMusicarta/

The MMYT Canon Project playlist: http://www.youtube.com/playlist?list=PL5JLvea_G1xc7Wkfo0zMiThrWW2yUgBEF

> Subscribe to MMYT for instant updates!

Musicarta SoundCloud: https://soundcloud.com/musicarta-com and the SoundCloud Canon playlist: https://soundcloud.com/musicarta-com/sets/the-canon-project-1

If you enjoy learning keyboard skills the Musicarta way, look into the following Musicarta digital home study downloads via the tabs on the main site navbar.

The Pyramids Variations – a fast-track triad-based repertoire builder and introduction to keyboard improvisation. (Also available from Amazon Books.)

Musicarta Key Chords Volume 1 – a methodical approach to building your keyboard chord vocabulary and developing your aural skills. (Amazon and Kindle.)

The Musicarta Canon Project – 2.0

Pachelbel's Canon in D major is the ideal place to start learning how to play – and play with! – chords at the keyboard. The Canon's simple chords repeat predictably under right hand melodic figures – the perfect conditions for learning about harmony, melody writing and improvisation.

Each module in the Musicarta Canon Project adds a 'bite-sized' piece to build your own unique performance, suggesting what to play and showing you how to practice.

Much-loved and highly adaptable, the Canon chord sequence forms the basis of numerous other pieces of popular music, and you will be able to apply the keyboard skills and theory learnt in this series of lessons to many other chord sequences going forward.

Studying the Canon also provides a great opportunity to develop your musical ear. Start learning to tell just by listening what chords are being used in mainstream popular music.

Great for ambitious young keyboard players, classical crossovers and adult piano re-starters/continuers. Perfect continuing education for semi-pro and pro musicians. An ideal supplement to traditional piano lessons – teaches theory and improvisation in an attractive, contemporary way.

This second edition of the Musicarta Canon Project contains full teaching notes to the 'Canon Diaries' entries which have been appearing on Mister Musicarta YouTube since the launch of the Canon Project.

These ongoing explorations of the Canon chord sequence demonstrate the kind of creative freedom you can expect to achieve if you study the Canon Project thoroughly and put what you have learnt into practice.

Purchase of this Amazon Books edition entitles user to the free download of supporting audio and MIDI files from webmaster@musicarta.com.

MUSICARTA A methodical approach to modern keyboard skills and repertoire.

Visit www.musicarta.com – your gateway to keyboard creativity!